# Powering the Net Zero Energy Transition

A Sustainable and Reliable Strategy using Molten Salt Reactors for Energy Prosperity

**By Clive Wilmer**

## DISCLAIMER

# Table of Contents

# Chapter 1
# Introduction

**H**ouston we have a problem! But this isn't an Apollo-13 type of problem, the kind of problem where you throw a few boffins at it for a couple of days. No this is a problem that will take sustained focus and investment over years. So, what is the issue? The UK will need to produce massive amounts of additional electricity —at least double what we currently generate, none of it from fossil fuels— and to do so reliably and efficiently, without producing huge quantities of greenhouse gases. This massive multi-decade undertaking is not being delivered and will not be achieved. Energy demand is continually increasing and improving production efficiency accelerates the issue.

Nobody wants to admit or face up to what this will mean because there is no *plan* (only some fanciful targets) —and it cannot be delivered just using wind and solar even with batteries.

Thomas Sowell said *"If you want to help people tell them the truth; if you want to help yourself tell them what they want to hear"*. Well, our politicians have been doing the latter for the past three decades, pretending that we can achieve the transition to net zero painlessly, cost-free and generate 'green jobs'. It is what we want to hear and believe—but reality? Not so much.

However, what if I told you there's a solution that offers abundant, reliable, safe, green, and cheap electricity that could solve this problem? Too good to be true, right? I believe such a solution exists—one that is both realistic and achievable. This book was written to share that solution with you. If you read to the end, we can turn scepticism, pessimism, and fear about the future into optimism—without ending up colder, poorer, and hungrier.

By now, you're probably thinking: He's going to start talking about nuclear power or fusion. Most people already have a view on nuclear power, and many fear it. They immediately dismiss any solution involving "nuclear" based on three main drawbacks:

1. Nuclear power isn't safe (e.g., Chernobyl, Fukushima, Three Mile Island).

2. Nuclear waste is dangerous and difficult to dispose of.

3. Nuclear proliferation—by-products can be used to make weapons.

The solution I propose has none of these issues. It's called a Molten Salt Reactor (MSR). At room temperature, salts are normally solid, but if heated sufficiently, they become liquid. An MSR is fundamentally different from a conventional pressurised water reactor (PWR). PWRs use water to cool the reactor, but to prevent the water from turning into steam, they operate at massive pressures. If the pressure becomes too high, the containment vessel could fail, causing an explosion, or hydrogen could build up and also explode. This is the root cause of the problems created by those disasters—a steam or hydrogen explosion resulting from water cooling in a pressurised environment.

In contrast, MSRs run at low pressure but high temperatures—similar to the pressure in a garden hose—and they cannot "explode." There is no steam, hydrogen, or other material that can explode in this way. If they leak, the hot liquid salt would simply cool and freeze back into a solid. If they get too hot, the liquid salt is passively drained—using gravity—into a drain tank, where the reaction cannot continue, and it naturally cools. In this context, "passive" means no external intervention is required; safety is inherent to the design.

On the second problem of waste, a traditional (PWR) large nuclear plant (1 Giga Watt electric - 1 GWe) produces 25-30 tonnes of high-level waste per year [1] or 3 cubic meters if the fuel is recycled. An MSR using the liquid salt fuel cycle produces only about 1% of this volume as it is much more efficient and burns up nearly all the raw fuel producing heat and therefore electricity. For comparison, a 1 GWe coal power plant produces 300,000 tonnes of ash and 6 million tonnes of $CO_2$ per year [2]. Furthermore, it takes 1,000 to 10,000 years for conventional (Uranium) high-level nuclear waste to return to the same levels of radioactivity as when it was mined. Waste from an MSR, however, takes only 300 years to reach background radiation levels, and after just 10 years, its radioactivity is reduced by 83% [3].

Lastly, MSRs do not produce plutonium—the material commonly used in nuclear weapons. MSRs can be "breeder" reactors, where thorium (or uranium) is added to sustain the reaction without needing expensive refuelling cycles where the reactor is shut down, the old fuel is removed and new fuel is added. However, to start the process for a new reactor you need to feed it some Uranium or Plutonium to start the reaction. This is beneficial because you can use old fuel from conventional reactors thus reducing the problem of old fuel waste. Alternatively, stocks of plutonium can also be consumed to start the process. Thus, building and starting an MSR can reduce the problem of nuclear waste and the risk of nuclear weapons proliferation.

In short, we can confidently refute those three common objections. Advanced nuclear reactors, such as MSRs, are inherently safe. We will explore this in more detail in a later chapter, where we'll address other concerns, such as transportation risks, terrorism, and potential radiation exposure in case of an accident. Having debunked the first three concerns, the next common objection people raise is the cost.

We're constantly told that wind and solar are great green generators that will keep the lights on and the country moving. We just need to build enough of them - right? The government targets are 50 gigawatts of offshore wind and 70 gigawatts of solar. For comparison purposes, 1 giga-watt is approximately enough electricity to power 1 million homes.

The major issue with these is that they are not reliable, they are intermittent depending on the wind or the sun. This means that alternative sources of power are required for when the sun doesn't shine (at night, or indeed much of the time in the UK - I know I have solar on my house) or the wind doesn't blow. This happens more frequently than we think, usually at inconvenient times on cold, still winter days. Keeping coal, gas, or oil-fired power (thermal) plants as a backup for just a few days a year is expensive. It is analogous to you keeping an extra spare car all year, with all the associated insurance, depreciation, tax and servicing (fixed) costs but only taking it out a couple of weekends when the sun is shining and you want to go to the seaside. Of course, unlike a car (where you jump in, start up and drive it away) a thermal power plant takes days to warm up and cool down. Generating companies receive massive payments for this.

Additionally, we end up paying owners of wind farms NOT to generate electricity so we don't overload the grid on windy days. These intermittent power sources are so problematic for the grid that battery technology must be deployed at scale and expense to mitigate this simply to manage the voltage and frequency fluctuations. The plans for wind have hinged on the assumption that costs will keep falling, whereas in 2023 the costs started to rise sharply. After no companies bid to build new wind farms, the UK chairman of RWE was quoted as saying the price paid to generators would need to increase by 70% [5] to £70 per MWh.  We the consumers are going to have to pick that up.

In the next chapter, we will look at all the issues with wind and solar in slightly more depth.

Let's return to the cost criticism levelled against nuclear power. We should consider the total cost of building the plant and also the cost of decommissioning it.  Running a conventional nuclear plant, compared to coal or gas plants, involves much lower ongoing fuel costs. However, large PWR plants, such as Hinkley Point C, are extremely expensive to build. Consumers and taxpayers will pay £92.50 per MWh (at 2012 prices) for the electricity produced by Hinkley Point C under the Contracts for Difference (CfD) arrangement. Sizewell C's price, if approved, will be £89.50 per MWh.

However, the price we pay is not the same as the cost.  The owners are being compensated for political and other risks via the guaranteed minimum price of electricity under the CfD.  The argument that costs will fall as more are built still leaves it looking expensive. Nonetheless, we paid (strike) prices of £115 per MWh under Contract for Difference (CfD) for the first offshore wind farms. In future chapters, we'll explore these CfD economics further, as they are crucial to understanding the relative costs of different power-generation solutions.

Even so, the National Audit Office concluded that up to six Hinkley-sized plants could have been built at the same cost to consumers/taxpayers if the British state had financed the project itself with government bonds[15]. Small modular reactors (SMRs) could offer a much cheaper solution. This is the ethos most companies developing MSR technology apply—small reactors that can be built at scale and delivered to the operating site.

In the end, I am pragmatic, if we can build a wind/solar infrastructure with sufficient power storage (e.g. batteries) and connect it to the grid at a lower cost than nuclear then let's do it. The problem is that there is no chance of this being viable with the current technologies. Many environmentalists and advocates argue it can be done, but it cannot. Lithium-ion batteries, for example, require vast amounts of rare earth metals, and the quantities needed vastly exceed known reserves. Costs will rise due to scarcity, and this is already happening.

Environmentalist's hopes rely on future advances in battery technology that are not simply a slightly better version but are an order of magnitude or two better. It would require an advance similar to the leap from transistors to silicon chips in computing. It may happen, there are promising developments, but it must become commercially available at scale and at a reasonable price. This is where the proponents of pie-in-the-sky thinking will try to convince us to simply hold out. They will talk the game up and use all kinds of forecasts to justify what is essentially inaction. That is not what a prudent society does with something as vital as the electricity supply.

The same argument applies to fusion. It's the ultimate silver bullet for our energy needs, but despite claims it could happen within the next decade, fusion has been "ten years away" for the past 30 years. Massive challenges remain, and Pareto's law applies: the last 20% of work takes 80% of the time.

If we level arguments of wishful thinking about solar, wind and fusion, what are the barriers to advanced nuclear, and where are the operating molten salt reactors?

China has been running a small developmental reactor since 2020, and it's progressing to a full-sized commercial one. Denmark and the US are developing similar reactors, and various UK universities and companies have projects in the early stages.

The US ran an MSR from 1965 until 1969 at Oak Ridge and they were ready to build a commercial-scale reactor. However, funding was cancelled because PWR were already available and they produced plutonium for nuclear weapons whereas a Thorium fueled MSR didn't. Something similar happened in the UK. At this time quantities of plutonium were required to fuel the American nuclear weapons programs and this was more pressing than efficient, effective and clean energy production.

There has been controversy in some countries over identifying nuclear energy as part of the transition to a net-zero future, even though fission reactors don't produce greenhouse gasses.    This controversy has arisen because they are not perceived as 'green' or renewable.    This comes back to the misconceptions over their safety and the issue of nuclear waste.    Challenging this perception and demonstrating that it should be heading up our list of energy solutions. MSR can deliver safe, abundant, cost-effective, greenhouse-gas-free energy within the same timescales that it takes to commission a new offshore wind farm (currently it takes 10 years) in the UK.

Cheap, reliable power is essential to the continuation of our society. Failure to deliver this is an existential risk.

# Chapter 2 Green Energy Transition

In this chapter, we will examine the problems with the current approach to achieving a "carbon-free" grid primarily using intermittent renewables. There is, of course, some argument over the necessity, wisdom, and speed of this transition, that as a society, we should move away from burning fossil fuels. Still, it appears the public is primarily settled on the matter. However, challenges arise when the costs of this process become significantly larger than the public has been prepared for. Until recently, this has been hidden in the slowly rising consumer bills to provide subsidies to renewable generators. In the UK in 2021, these subsidies amounted to about 20% of electricity bills, but the fact that this has been phased in over 12 years has masked the impact until now.

In 2022, Russia invaded Ukraine, and all hell broke loose in the energy markets. Natural gas prices skyrocketed, which in turn hit electricity prices. Cue panic among politicians (and the media) as they realise how much we depend on cheap energy. It was then that cracks in the consensus began to appear.

*"A future of abundant and clean energy will help to boost our economic prosperity, attract future investment, and support our industrial heartlands. The cheaper our energy, the greater*

*the competitive advantage we have."* Grant Shapps, the UK Energy Security Secretary [7]

This would be an about-turn from subsidising renewables and loading the cost onto consumers and assuming that "this future" is ever acted upon, which is seriously doubtful. If we are committed to reducing the share of fossil fuels used to generate electricity, we must ensure that this can be done at reasonable costs, not too far removed from those we currently pay in 2023 (which are already significantly elevated compared to those we 'enjoyed' in 2021).

The major problem is the complete fallacy of the argument that wind and solar are efficient, cost-effective solutions to decarbonise the grid. It is beyond doubt that they can only achieve this aim with other technology to back them up and at enormous cost. The reason for this is the problem of intermittency—variable output beyond our control. The sun shines or doesn't, and the wind either blows or not. Overcoming intermittency problems will require other solutions that will drive costs to prohibitive levels. The more we rely on intermittent renewables, the larger the capacity we need in reserve to cover the inevitable gaps in supply.

## The Rising Cost of Renewables

The assumption from governments, regulators, and the green lobby is that the cost of renewables (intermittent resources) will fall as production volumes ramp up and technology improves. Indeed, this has been the case until recently. Solar panels have halved in cost over the past 5 to 7 years due to mass production in China. China is already producing solar panels several times the world's demand every year and dumping the excess into international markets, so prices will probably keep falling, albeit more slowly. Wind, especially offshore wind, is a different story.

Wind turbines have become much bigger and more efficient, and the guaranteed price paid to scheme operators for their electricity kept falling until 2022. As we alluded to in the introduction, there are reasons to believe that costs will not continue falling. Wind turbines are already close to their maximum theoretical efficiency—the Betz limit—and their effectiveness will always be determined by the wind available. For wind turbines to supply only the annual global growth in demand, nearly 350,000 would need to be built yearly. This is 1.5 times as many as have been built since the early 2000s and would require more land than the area of the British Isles every year.

According to Wikipedia, the UK currently (in 2023) has 15 GW of onshore and 15 GW of offshore wind through 11,000 turbines [8]. For the UK to reach the government target of 50 GW of offshore wind by 2030, we must build another 35 GW. Working out how many more turbines and wind farms would be needed is subject to many factors, as the size of turbines has been increasing, rendering some historical comparisons inaccurate. Therefore, we can base our calculations on helpful information from Equinor, which is building a massive wind farm at Dogger Bank. This will produce 3.6 GW of electricity from 277 enormous 260-metre-tall turbines (each producing around 13 MW) [9]. We would need another nine gigantic wind farms to hit the target. However, this project is three times the size of the previous largest wind farm, Hornsea 1, which was around 1.2 GW. The difficulty is that it takes up to 10 years from conception to implementation, mainly due to environmental, regulatory, and planning constraints. In June 2023, there were 98 GW of offshore wind projects at every stage of development: operational, under construction, consented, or planned [10]. So, we should be able to hit this target; however, the installation rate will need to triple, which is a big ask as there are many potential bottlenecks. Furthermore, timescales interact with challenges in the supply chain and grid connections.

UK ports will need significant investment to service the required volume (and size) of equipment. Offshore wind requires specialist ships to lift the turbines into position; the lead time on these ships is three to four years, and they are in increasing demand from the US and Europe, leading to potential bottlenecks in capable shipyards. Tripling the installation rate will also require a commensurate uplift in the skilled workforce, which is excellent from a short-term jobs perspective but will be a strain to deliver within the timescales and will ultimately create overcapacity and subsequent redundancies.

The UK is surrounded by seas with brilliant wind conditions, much of them in relatively accessible, shallow waters. However, as seabed leasing advances, the availability of these perfect locations decreases, forcing development further out to sea, requiring longer transit times and more complex installation in deeper waters.

So far, so good—but this brings us to the question of cost and whether many of these projects will proceed. During the third Contracts for Difference (CfD) auction round (2020), projects achieved a UK record low of £39.65 per MWh, a 30% price drop from the £57.50 per MWh seen in the second CfD round auction in 2017 [11]. However, there were no bidders in the latest round (2023), which set a price cap of less than £45 per MWh. None. It gets worse—within a few months, several significant developers pulled the plug on large wind farm projects as it was no longer economical to proceed with the investment. Major power projects require massive upfront investment, relying on steady returns over the operational life (only 15 to 20 years for wind). The government estimates that £54bn of capital investment will be needed by 2030 to meet its target.

There are three primary reasons behind this change in circumstances. Firstly, interest rates have risen dramatically over the past two years, reaching 25-year highs. Financing costs have a considerable impact on the economic viability of such projects due to the reduced value of future cash flows through the discount rate that must be applied, thus rendering some projects without a viable return. Secondly, inflation has been rampant, especially in the wind turbine sector, where manufacturers were producing turbines at a loss. Production losses were exacerbated by higher-than-forecast repair costs, which were a liability for the manufacturers (Siemens is reporting a $16bn exposure). This could not continue indefinitely, so prices will have to rise, and with worldwide demand buoyant, this trend is set to continue for a while. This brings us to previously quoted remarks from the UK chairman of RWE that prices would need to rise to £70 per MWh. The latest proposal from the UK government is now to set a strike price of £73 per MWh [20]. It is also likely that various planned projects from previous auctions, like Orsted's Hornsea 3, will receive an improved strike price so that they can proceed.

*"Conditions are extremely challenging across the whole industry right now, with a supply chain squeeze, increasing prices and cost of capital, and fiscal frameworks not reflecting current market realities."* Vattenfall CEO Anna Borg [12].

Is it possible that these costs will decline? Currently, one-third of the cost of wind turbines is in the raw materials, especially the various metals used to manufacture them. Copper, lithium, nickel, cobalt, and rare earth elements are essential components. These metals will be in increasing demand as the world pursues the same strategies for decarbonisation. This demand far outstrips the known and planned resources for mining and refining these materials. The average time to open a new mine from discovery to operation is 16 years, so given the rapid acceleration in demand, we can expect to see sharp rises in prices. These will not be short-lived spikes but sustained increases.

"IEA transition policies would cause metal prices to reach historical peaks for an unprecedented sustained period of over a decade," IMF [16].

We can safely assume this is now a floor rather than a ceiling for wind projects. Rising costs will have to be considered alongside the issue of intermittency and overcapacity. Intermittency must be mitigated by backup generation, and overcapacity is when the network is overwhelmed. We have to pay wind farm owners **not** to supply electricity to the grid because we cannot use or store it. This means that when they talk about a price of £70 per MWh, it is not the actual cost to consumers. We need to add the cost of backup generation or (battery) storage, known as balancing reserves, and the cost of expanding the grid to the North and Scotland.

A minor but important point is that most (around 90%) of the metals required for wind turbines and lithium-ion batteries are refined and processed in China. The majority of solar PV panels are produced in China. The raw materials for batteries are processed and manufactured in China, too. In a nutshell, there is also an energy security issue with simply relying on renewables and batteries, partly what politicians reference when discussing energy security. The Chinese state is authoritarian and fond of using leverage to achieve its goals. It could exploit this vulnerability if it chose to do so. China is already using supplies of germanium in its trade and political disputes with the United States.

The decisions made regarding the UK's energy mix have been based on the assumption that the cost of offshore wind, solar, and batteries has fallen and will continue to decline. However, that assumption, particularly about wind and batteries, has been undermined. That is another reason to review our path.

## Managing Renewable Intermittency

Even though out at sea wind speeds are more consistent, they still only operate for 91% of the time (8% there is too little wind, and 1% too much - based on data from the North Sea). [14] That means we need that backup 10% of the time, often when we need peak power - on cold, windless winter days or during storms.  We know solar won't pick up the slack in winter (apart from a few hours). When weather systems arise that result in a lack of wind, they often afflict the whole country or even larger areas.  This could make it harder to import electricity from the continent, which may be suffering similar conditions and is also beginning to rely heavily on intermittent sources.

How do you plan for this in terms of capacity? Do we need balancing reserves for the entire wind capacity onshore and offshore (c. 65 GW)? Well, obviously not, but the answer is not straightforward. As the percentage of power generated by intermittent sources increases, the capacity credit (the measure of the amount of power we can rely on) decreases. In circumstances where we get 20% of our power from intermittent resources, we need up to 20% of this capacity to be supported by available balancing power. Some studies suggest a linear relationship, so if 80% of our power came from wind/solar and that intermittent power was 40 GW, we would need 32GW (80% of 40 GW) of balancing power to be available. However, this hasn't been empirically tested anywhere with loads over 20-30%. Also, such a test must be specific and relevant to UK conditions.

However, the sheer scale of the daily fluctuations in wind and solar energy available is genuinely terrifying (see Figure 1 below). We are overbuilding capacity to make up for the variability, but then we will still have to back it up with other sources. Plus, we have to deal with the excesses by paying people not to overload the grid. It must be the most inefficient (expensive) way to build a resilient electricity grid system.

| 24hr Avg supply (GW) | Tues | Wed | Thur | Fri | Sat | Sun | Mon | 12/12/ 2023 19:15 |
|---|---|---|---|---|---|---|---|---|
| Fossil Fuels | 17.8 | 21.9 | 14.1 | 12.8 | 3.8 | 6.1 | 14 | 22.5 |

| Renewables | 9.5 | 7.9 | 19.2 | 14.8 | 18.5 | 15.2 | 10.4 | 6.92 |
|---|---|---|---|---|---|---|---|---|
| Nuclear and Bio | 7.6 | 7.7 | 7.7 | 7.6 | 6.2 | 6.3 | 6.8 | 7.65 |
| Transfers | 1.9 | 0 | -3 | 0.2 | 4.1 | 4.3 | 3.5 | 3.3 |

**Figure 1.** National Grid - a representative week December 2023 (GW)

In Figure 2, we can begin to see the issue. On Tuesday, renewable sources generated 9.5 GW; on Thursday, they more than doubled this at 19.2 GW. I took a snapshot, and they were only providing 6.92 GW. The minimum amount of electricity generated by wind in any one 30-minute period (from 1st April 2023 to 12th December 2023) was a miserable 78.42 MW; the maximum amount was a stonking 16,540.5 MW. For the lowest 24-hour period (on 16th August), wind generated an average of 1.01 GW. If we didn't have gas-fired stations, how would we cope with this variability  - it is not even matched to demand - it is as random as the wind. Demand is often rising, and wind power is dropping or vice versa.

How do we answer the question: (if) we require 1 GW of continuous power output (in the UK), how much wind/solar and (battery) storage do we need to deploy? The answer is that it depends on cost.

If you overbuild the wind and solar, you need less storage capacity.

I managed to retrieve some information from Sweden regarding the weather, where they have similar Winter periods of anti-cyclonic gloom (no wind and low sun) [49].   To produce 1GW of reliable power, they start by deploying 3GW of wind (onshore) and 3GW of solar; this creates the need for 550 GW of battery storage, which is an immense amount due to the long Dankflaute in November / December 2023 (real-world data). Even with this amount of storage, it was only partially recharged at the end of the period, so another prolonged period of low wind (in January) would rapidly deplete it.

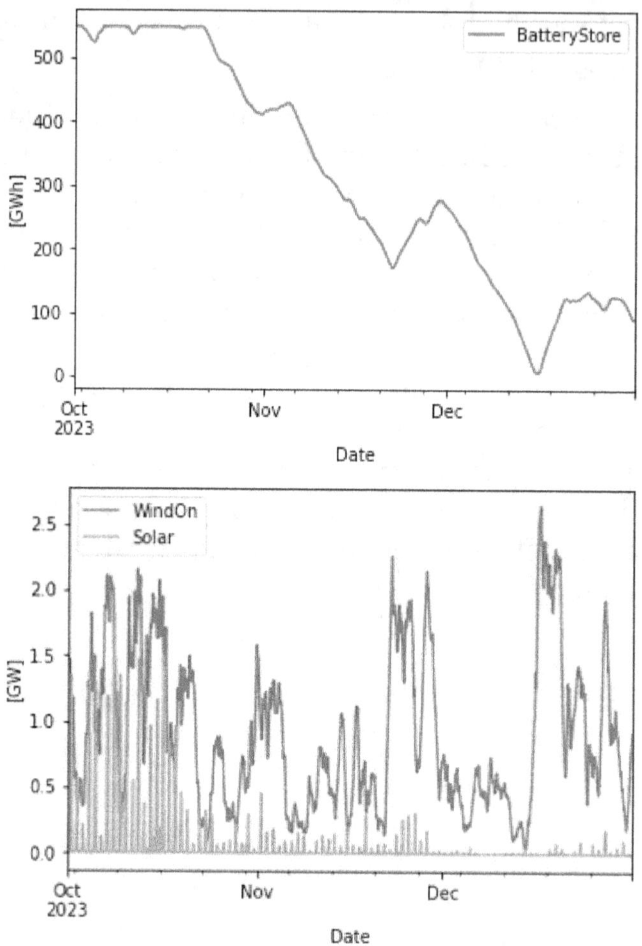

**Figure 2.** [49] Swedish 1GW Output from Wind/Solar and Battery (3GW instal)

Over-installing wind and solar up to 6 GW each reduced the need for battery storage to 130 GWh, which is still incredibly high. However, because wind and solar are less expensive than battery storage, the overall cost of the 3GW installation is still reduced. When we optimise the mix of wind/

solar and batteries to minimise the cost, solar energy is almost entirely squeezed out of the mix because of its low productivity during winter.

Companies will only install 'excess' capacity if they are remunerated for doing so. Even if the excess capacity is used to produce green hydrogen to store excess wind for use during periods of low wind/ solar, companies will still need to make the same return on the wind turbines used to do that as they will on one that is fully utilised.

## Balancing the Grid

The reason that balancing the grid is so important is that it is susceptible to disruption. The voltage cannot deviate without damage to components or threatening the supply altogether. If there is sudden extra demand on the grid, then this will cause the voltage to begin to drop, and additional supply must be added, and vice versa. Failure to do so very promptly can result in the complete failure of part of the grid, which can spread rapidly to other parts unless isolated. This causes blackouts - when a whole section of the grid trips out, causing a failure to supply industry, services, hospitals, and homes.

To manage very short, minor-term variations in the grid voltage/ frequency, the National Grid operator (ESO) has a number of options open to deployment, including special capacitors, batteries, and flywheels (which store energy) that can be quickly engaged to drive generators.

Part of the issue with wind and solar power is that small-scale things like solar panels on your roof or small onshore wind farms are not regulated by the grid. The grid operator has no control over these elements, and indeed, they appear to the grid as negative demand when they are producing power into the grid, and demand appears to drop. This all complicates the picture for the ESO.

Analysis by Public First predicts that the UK's demand for power will exceed baseload capacity by 7.5GW at peak times by 2028, a shortfall equivalent to the power used by more than 7 million homes." [30] The more intermittent power we have, the more we will have to subsidise balancing power sources for doing nothing for longer because they will have less offsetting electricity sales. Overall, more capacity will need to be set aside to meet spikes in demand or dips in supply as the overall proportion of wind and solar energy increases.

The problem in accepting this approach is that the vast majority of the balancing power is currently provided by fossil fuels, operating increasingly old and inefficient infrastructure. Some capacity is being added through batteries, but this is primarily suited to fulfilling short spikes in demand, such as evening peaks. Otherwise, mass battery storage is very expensive and has a relatively short lifespan before it must be replaced. This leaves a problem that will become increasingly evident as we reach the 2030s - how do we reliably plug the balancing gap and eliminate fossil fuels from the equation?

If you think I am being alarmist and there is nothing to worry about, then simply note that consumers (not just industry) are paid to use less electricity at specific peak periods (usually from dusk onwards on windless days). British winters are renowned for having lengthy periods of intense cold and low winds caused when zones of atmospheric high pressure settle over the country. The phenomenon is known as "Dunkelflaute" in Germany but is more commonly referred to by meteorologists as anticyclonic gloom. These periods can last several days or even weeks. The more we rely on wind and solar power, which the weather can disrupt, the worse the risk becomes. Under these conditions, we rely on gas-powered stations for two-thirds of our electricity, with nuclear, biomass and importing electricity via interconnectors making up the rest.

An over-reliance on wind and solar is the most complicated method of building an energy grid because they are inherently unreliable and have no corresponding ability to adjust to the level of demand. Power generating capability that can be varied according to demand is known as load following.

## The Capacity Market

The UK is now subsidising existing thermal power plants (coal, gas and oil) to remain open. To regulate this and provide a balancing function, the UK Government created the "Capacity Market", which aims to reduce the risk of future electricity blackouts during periods of low wind and high demand. The Capacity Market makes subsidy payments to reliable electricity generators to ensure electricity generation is available during system stress. The payments are intended to encourage investment in new *reliable* capacity and incentivise existing capacity to remain open.

Capacity Market payments are paid regardless of whether a plant produces electricity.  It is guaranteed income for the producer, in addition to the sale of any electricity produced. Auctions take place to determine which combination of new and existing capacity will meet the system requirement at the lowest cost to consumers.  Nearly all required capacity for a specific year is procured at auction four years in advance – this allows sufficient time to build any required new capacity. These auctions are referred to as "T-4" auctions.

The cost of this subsidy has risen every year over the past four years [21] see Figure 4.

| Auction year | Delivery Year | Cost (per KWy) | Capacity | Annual Cost |
|---|---|---|---|---|
| 2019 | 2023-24 | £15.97 | 4.4 GW | £70.3m |
| 2020 | 2024-25 | £18.00 | 4.1 GW | £73m |

| 2021 | 2025-26 | £30.59 | 4.2 GW | £129m |
| 2022 | 2026-27 | £63.00 | 4.3 GW | £271m |
| 2023 | 2027-28 | £65.00 | 7.5 GW | £2.8bn |

**Figure 4.** T-4 auction subsidies for reliable balancing power

Note that some of the capacity bought in the T-4 auctions runs over multiple years (up to 15), so the cumulative capacity and cost are increasing year on year.

New government data shows that consumers will have £2.8bn added to their bills in 2028—about £100 per household—to pay power station owners and battery providers to provide balancing capacity. With the new Government's determination to phase out all fossil fuels by 2030, we must assume that the cost of balancing the grid will have to fall primarily on pumped storage, batteries, or even hydrogen.

Currently, the cheapest and most effective form of balancing reserves would be open-cycle natural gas (OCGT) plants. These can start up relatively quickly, taking the time from burning fuel to generating electricity. They are also designed to run at variable and low loads. Coal thermal power plants typically take 6 to 12 hours (or longer) to come online (and a proportion of these start-ups fail), so they are less suited to this role. Combined cycle natural gas plants (CCGT) are the most efficient in absolute terms but are designed to run at full load and are typically larger (thus more expensive) than OCGT plants.

The UK currently has about 10 OCGT (1.2 GW) and  32 CCGT plants producing about 28 GW [17]; some of these are now approaching 30 years old (the expected lifespan).   The operators of CCGT plants are now faced with the prospect that their plants will usually be idle. This makes it harder to sustain profitable operations, especially for older plants that are likely to have higher operating costs near the end of their life. However, these types of plants will certainly be required to fulfil a balancing role. Again, given the government's position, there will be little incentive to spend excess amounts on maintenance to prolong the life or build a new plant.

## Extending and Expanding Grid Capacity

The last point to note is that with offshore wind, there is no power transmission infrastructure to support the new wind farms. Many wind farms are in places not easily connected to the existing grid. We need to build onshore 'collection' facilities that convert the DC power to AC  and then the transmission lines over land or undersea to carry the power onward to the final consumers. This means a vast and unprecedented level of investment in the National Grid, which is currently forecast to cost £11 billion. These costs will rise substantially, like every significant civil project. The costs are passed along to us, the electricity consumers, through higher bills.

Additionally, we have just had the news that to overcome political opposition, we will bribe people near new power transmission lines with reduced electric bills, costing £1,000 per year. The estimated cost of this is another £4bn, which again will be passed on to us as consumers.

Finally, as if all of that wasn't enough, in 2022, we had to pay the owners of wind farms £220mn NOT to generate electricity because we had too much wind (and solar) coming from the Northern part of the grid. Furthermore, when a wind farm is required to reduce output North of a grid constraint, another generator - almost always a flexible CCGT gas-fired generator - is necessary to increase output to the south of that constraint to make up the shortfall in energy and to correct the level of the reserve available on the system. It is difficult to project the future level of constraint payments, as these are known, but this will surely increase as the mix of renewables increases. However, if we are about to triple the amount of wind power, then we can safely say it will more than triple the cost as the overloading will become more frequent.

## The Real Cost of Wind

To work out the actual cost of wind power, we need to add the price we will pay for the electricity, the cost of subsidies for balancing energy, the upgrades to the grid, and the cost of payments for not producing it.

For the grid upgrades, that is £11bn + £4bn = £15bn (assuming financing and discounting are already applied). For the constraint payments to prevent the grid from being overloaded, we will assume £1bn, which I believe will be conservative.

£16 bn / 3017 TWh usable electricity - based on 28,000 MW (new wind capacity) over 30 years @ 41% average efficiency (EWEA figures [19]) = £5.30 per MWh.

In addition, we need to add the cost of the balancing reserves bought in the capacity market. Remember, this is a payment to provide capacity, and payment for electricity would be on top at the prevailing market rate. Based on the 2024 auction, that is £65 KWy, which is already £7.42 per MWh. This is very conservative, as the numbers have been rising yearly. I am not sure how it will work with the new government's target to decarbonise the grid by 2030, so presumably, fossil fuel-burning plants won't be eligible beyond this as the amount of intermittent renewables rises, so the cost of providing balancing power will increase sharply as we have to use batteries or hydrogen, which is several times more expensive. Therefore, I am going to extrapolate the rises to 2031/2 when the latest offshore wind comes on stream and also allow for increased use of batteries as cheaper fossil-fueled plants are phased out, which indicates prices of £76 KWy or £8.67 MWh.

Therefore, if we take the latest forecast strike prices for CfD of £73 MWh and add the balancing subsidies plus the additional grid costs (£5.30), then add the cost of providing "balancing power" at £8.67 (this is a minimum) we can see that the latest true cost of offshore wind will come in at least £87 MWh.

The strike price of the CfD is guaranteed by the UK Treasury (but will be passed on to consumers) and is inflation-linked. Remember this cost when we compare it to the cost of molten salt reactors, and you hear people say that nuclear power is expensive. It is already looking quite close to the price we would pay for power from a 3rd  Hinckley / Sizewell PWR, let alone the cost if we financed this more efficiently through the UK government.

That is before we get to the lower-cost claims for molten salt and small module reactors.

## Are Batteries or Hydrogen the answer?

Before moving on, we should discuss battery storage's role in balancing the grid. Batteries can be charged when the grid has excess supply from renewable sources during low demand, possibly at night (from wind) or in the middle of the day (from solar). The grid also suffers sharp spikes in demand, typically between 5 pm and 7 pm, and other brief interludes. Batteries can discharge their stored power relatively quickly, so they are helpful in fulfilling brief spikes in demand - but then, once discharged, cannot play a role until recharged. This limits their utility because they cannot easily meet sustained demand when sources of power from renewables are low, as they cannot be recharged.

Another factor is cost. Lithium-ion battery storage can be expensive compared to solar and wind, as it uses many rare earths and other materials. These costs are likely to stay relatively high due to the pressure on sources of these materials in terms of mining and refining them.

Recent developments in battery storage technology have made advances with long-duration redox flow batteries. These batteries are more flexible with a longer lifespan than (conventional) Lithium-ion batteries. They are unsuitable for cars and small portable devices because they have a much lower energy storage density. I.e. They are relatively big and heavy. However, this doesn't matter (as much) for grid storage/backup. Many versions of batteries use vanadium and toxic electrolytes to store power. This has many problems with other rare earth metals used in Lithiu-ion batteries, such as cobalt.

However, at least one company (ESS) has developed an iron that usesversion. This does not have any scarce, toxic or costly components. The company claims that once manufacturing is fully ramped up, they can provide power at around £50 to £60 (Levelised cost of ownership) per MWh based on continuous charge and discharge cycles. The batteries can discharge energy back to the grid for more extended periods (up to 12 hours), and don't suffer performance degradation over time, like Lithium-ion.

So far, so promising. However, this cost is on top of what the grid would have to pay the wind or solar generator for the power in the first place. So, the power delivered from the wind to the battery back to the grid would cost £130 to £140 per MWh. Each of their battery units can store 400 KWh released at 74Kw and is approximately 30 $M^2$. the size of a shipping container (12.2M x2.4M x 2.9M)

The second problem is the sheer scale of the storage we would need once there are no fossil fuels. Take a typical scenario of Dankelflaute — or anti-cyclonic gloom — in winter, where there is virtually no wind for four days ( a frequent scenario). Periods over a week have been happening often. In 2050 (our net zero target), our daily power demand is estimated to roughly double or 90 GW [7] per hour. There will be only one or perhaps two nuclear power stations, Hinckley C and Sizewell, generating approximately 7 GW). To cover four days of no wind and little solar, we need:

Total UK Demand for 4 days= 4 days x 24 hours x 90 GW = 8,640 GWh

Deduct solar generation from this amount, which in winter is only generating a few hours per day at low efficiency, say (3h @ 35% of 70 GW x 4 days is) 290 GWh.

Also deduct current nuclear power  (7GW x 24h x 4 days) = 672 GWh

Therefore, the total required battery storage = 7,678 GWh

We will need 19,195,000 shipping container-sized batteries to meet that demand from batteries. Assuming they are stacked five high, they would take up 115.17 million square metres or 115 square kilometres.  Each battery warehouse will also need to be connected to the grid.

The cost estimate I provided earlier was based on spreading the capital cost over continuous usage. This would be different for that capacity, which would mostly be sat idle. Currently, battery storage is about \$300 per KWh - assuming costs would fall to (even as low as) £100 per KWh, the total would be £767.8 Bn. That is for the most promising mass battery storage technology.

Finally, just a word about hydrogen. Using hydrogen as a source of stored energy to balance the grid is possible. Generate green hydrogen from renewable power sources when there is excess power over demand. Then, when the situation is reversed, you burn the hydrogen in a thermal plant to produce electricity. The problem once again is cost. You need an extensive capital investment in excess wind and solar capacity. The plant needs to produce the hydrogen, and then you need another generator system to turn it into electricity. If the requirement is to meet 40 GW of demand, you will need to have almost this amount of generating capacity from hydrogen because wind and solar will be developing next to nothing. High levels of capital investment can only be justified when employed efficiently and at a high utilisation rate. This is still cheaper than lithium-based batteries, but it also tells us that it has yet to be deployed anywhere.

This is the essential issue at the heart of the renewables lie. Whenever you install capacity that needs to be continuous and reliable, it must be backed up by other means of generating electricity. It was no big deal when that backup was old fossil fuel power stations that had already been built and paid for. They could sit around saving money by NOT burning coal or gas. No one cared much. But what are the options when you can't use these or they don't exist? We sit around in the cold with torches and candles OR build nuclear power stations. We have to build nuclear power stations anyway, so why are we building and paying for all these renewables?

# Chapter 3
# Understanding Fission

From Chapter 2, we learned that we cannot rely solely on intermittent power sources, even those backed by batteries. To fully move away from fossil fuels, we need a source of electricity that is carbon-free (green, if you like), reliable, technically achievable in the next ten to fifteen years, and economical.

The reality is that decisions about the way forward need to be made today. Ten years to develop new capacity based on new designs is a short amount of time. You can build a new CCGT plan in three or four years, but even a new wind farm takes ten years to deliver. This time frame rules out relying on fusion power. Fusion is still in the laboratory, whatever the hopes are for the future. Even when the fundamental issues are solved, commercialising, and licensing will take many years. I don't think regulators will rush to approve the designs for a captive miniature sun (fusion). Fusion enthusiasts see it as a "silver bullet" for energy problems. Still, history tells us that despite the big claims, you should not gamble on this for something as essential to our lives as the electrical supply.

Realistically, the only solution to our energy needs is nuclear fission. The most significant barriers to this are political rather than technical. To recap, the four main objections are safety, radioactive waste, nuclear weapons, and cost. This chapter will be dedicated to backing up the assertions we made in chapter one about these issues and improving the understanding of the fundamentals. The cost issue(s) we will address in a later chapter

## Nuclear safety

It is fair to say that there is a generalised belief that nuclear power is particularly dangerous or inherently unsafe. The fact that radiation is silent, invisible, potentially deadly and can be cancer-causing gives rise to this concern. While this is true, we (humans) are not generally good at assessing this type of risk where the probability of our exposure is more or less non-existent. Unease, not to say fear, tends to make us shy away from the risk. The following table (figure 3 [22]) shows that many more people die from fossil fuels, including deaths from air pollution, than from generating nuclear power. It is almost the safest power source compared to the amount of energy it generates; only solar is marginally safer. In case anyone thinks I am trying to pull a fast one, this information includes all the deaths from nuclear accidents (e.g. Chornobyl and Fukushima).

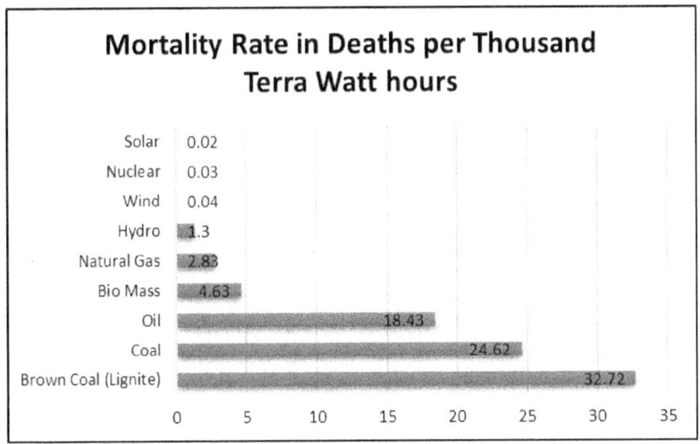


Figure 3. [22]

# Understanding Radiation

Radioactivity, also known as nuclear decay, radioactive decay, or nuclear disintegration, is the process by which an unstable atomic nucleus loses energy by emitting sub-atomic particles (radiation). A substance containing unstable nuclei is considered radioactive. The most common types of radiation are alpha, beta, and gamma decay. Alpha decay is a helium nucleus with very little range or penetration due to its size and is the least dangerous. Beta decay can simplistically be thought of as an electron or positron, and it has a short range but a small penetrative capacity. Modest protective measures are sufficient to stop alpha and beta radiation. Gamma radiation is electromagnetic radiation, simplistically a photon, is highly penetrative and the most likely to cause damage to human tissue and is, therefore, the most dangerous. The power of gamma radiation varies from a few kiloelectronvolts to approximately eight megaelectronvolts, depending on the source.

Radioactive decay is a random (i.e. stochastic) process at the level of single atoms. It is impossible to predict when a particular atom will decay. However, the overall decay rate can be expressed as a decay constant or half-life for a significant number of identical atoms. The half-lives of radioactive atoms have a vast range: from almost instantaneous to longer than the universe's age. Contrary to what you might think, isotopes with short half-lives decay faster, thus giving off more radiation than isotopes with long half-lives. Isotopes are distinct nuclear species of the same chemical element. They have the same atomic number and position in the periodic table but differ in nucleon numbers due to different numbers of neutrons in their nuclei.

The decaying nucleus is called the parent radionuclide, and the process produces at least one daughter nuclide. Except for gamma decay, the decay is a (nuclear) transmutation resulting in a daughter atom containing a different number of protons or neutrons (or both). When the number of protons changes, an atom of a different chemical element is created. It is important to note and understand this when considering the nuclear fuel cycle and by-products of the fission process.

We are surrounded by background radioactivity all the time in varying quantities. It is the quantity and type that is important. Relatively high levels of background radiation are found in some of the most densely inhabited places, but we mostly go about our business without concern. For example, Rome has similar levels of background radiation to that found around the site of the Fukushima nuclear plant post-accident. However, the latter area was evacuated, even though living in Rome is not considered particularly harmful to human health.

Thorium and uranium are elements that occur naturally in substantial quantities and are used in nuclear reactors. These elements are part of a series of actinides from the seventh row of the periodic table. All actinides are radioactive and release energy upon radioactive decay. The radioactive decay of uranium produces transient amounts of actinium and protactinium, and atoms of neptunium and plutonium are occasionally produced from transmutation reactions in uranium ores. The other actinides are purely synthetic elements.

Uranium and thorium also have diverse current or historical uses, and americium is used in the ionisation chambers of most modern smoke detectors.

## Nuclear Reactor Basics - Nuclear fission

The heart of a nuclear reactor, referred to as its core, will take fissile material and produce heat as a by-product of atomic decay. It is the fission — splitting of a nucleus that releases energy. That heat is ultimately used to generate electricity, similar to how a thermal gas power plant produces electricity.

Fissile material means that it is capable of sustaining a nuclear chain reaction - nuclear fission. In nuclear fission, the neutrons given off by radioactive decay collide with other unstable nuclides in the fissile material to emit more neutrons, thus sustaining the reaction. Each time a neutron is released, so is radiation energy in the form of heat. This process changes the atom, releasing the neutron to a more stable isotope. When referring to "burning" fuel in a nuclear reactor, we are talking about changing to another isotope. Nothing is actually burned in the usual sense of the word. It is just a way of thinking about how the fissile material is consumed while producing heat that is analogous to burning.

## The Neutron Economy

When we think of nuclear fission, we all think of the pictures of atomic explosions. Actually, it is difficult to sustain nuclear fission. Nuclear weapons are deliberately engineered to release their energy at once and are very difficult to make (fortunately), which is why proliferation has been contained. Many things will prevent or cause a fission chain reaction to stop. If this weren't the case, the naturally occurring uranium and thorium would be in a continuous state of fission. The chain reaction stops if a neutron is released but does not collide with another atomic nucleus to release further neutrons.

Neutrons are uncharged, which allows them to penetrate deep into an atom and close to the nuclei, thus scattering neutrons by nuclear forces. Thorium needs to receive a neutron before it becomes fissile. It is stable in its natural state, as is most (97%) naturally occurring uranium.

The more energy—the faster—a released neutron is travelling, the less likely it is to collide with a nucleus and continue the reaction, although the greater the probability that it will fission when it does. Note that this relationship is very important in reactor design.

In many reactors, adding a "moderating" material is necessary to slow down the neutrons and cause them to "bounce about", thus increasing the chance of hitting another nucleus.  Graphite is frequently used as a moderating material because it will not absorb the neutrons.  However, a great many materials can be used as moderators. Conversely, some reactor designs include the moderator within the fuel carrier mix; they do not require structural moderators in the reactor core. The advantage of this approach is that graphite or other structural moderators eventually become irradiated.

The fission reaction must generate at least as many neutrons as are absorbed or escaped /wasted (so greater than one). The number of neutrons generated by nuclear fuel being fissioned is known as the neutron yield.  The probability of a neutron hitting a nucleus is called the (neutron induced)   cross-section,   and   the   yield   is determined by the cross-section and the energy of the colliding neutron (measured in electron volts (eV).

The neutron economy of a reactor drives many of the design considerations. The fission reaction is sensitive to fuel type and temperature. If the reaction sustains itself, it is said to be critical.

## The raw material

### Uranium

Uranium is the most common fuel for reactors. Most naturally occurring uranium is not fissile, which means it cannot support a nuclear chain reaction needed to power a nuclear reactor. It needs to be processed to turn it into fissile material so that the Uranium isotope 235 (U-235) can be isolated and concentrated away from Uranium-238, known as enrichment. Only 0.3% of the naturally occurring uranium is U-235. It is the only naturally occurring fissile isotope. Uranium-238 (U-238) is fertile; that is it can be made fissile (ready to be "burned" in a nuclear reaction), and it can be transmuted to fissile plutonium-239 by receiving a neutron. U-238 is only fissionable by fast neutrons, though with a small cross-section - hence, a lower probability of this occurring. Uranium-235, and to a lesser degree, uranium-233, have a much higher fission cross-section for slow neutrons. The cross-section is like the probability of a neutron hitting the target, the nucleus of another atom. The relative cross-section to slow or fast neutrons will become relevant when discussing different reactors.

When thermal neutrons (i.e., neutrons that a moderator has slowed down) hit, the neutron can be captured by the U-238 nucleus to transmute the uranium into U-239, which rapidly decays into Neptunium-239, which in turn decays into Plutonium-239.

## Plutonium

Plutonium (Pu) does not occur naturally (in any quantity); it can only happen through nuclear fission. For example, when U-238 receives a neutron, it becomes Pu-239.  Pu-239 is highly fissile, making it a very suitable material for reactors.  However, because it does not occur naturally, it is usually only used as a small proportion of a fuel mix added to enrich it. Plutonium 239 has a thermal neutron cross-section larger than U-235, making it more likely to fission.

The most common use for plutonium is in nuclear weapons.  It is usually created by burning Uranium fuel rods in pressurised water reactors, it is then separated from the spent fuel rods during reprocessing.

The UK is currently storing about 140 tonnes of Plutonium.  If this were burned in molten salt reactors, it would produce enough power for the *entire* electric grid for *fifty* years.  This would reduce or remove the cost of storing it and remove it as a weapons proliferation threat.  To kick start

Thorium-Uranium, you need a highly fissile material like Plutonium. For a 1 GW Thorium MSR reactor, you would need circa. Eight tonnes of plutonium or uranium (223 or 235). This is like sitting on an energy gold mine if we choose to use it, and why wouldn't we? It is not doing anything constructive at the moment.

## Thorium

Named after Thor, the god of thunder in Norse mythology, Thorium is a silver-coloured, slightly radioactive metal found in igneous rocks and heavy mineral sands. It is up to four times more abundant in nature than uranium but historically has seen little use in industry or power generation. Thorium-232, the only naturally occurring isotope of thorium, is not fissile but fertile. It requires high-energy neutrons to undergo fission — the splitting of atomic nuclei, which releases energy for electricity generation. When irradiated (receiving a neutron), Thorium-232 becomes Protactinium-233, which quickly decays to become Uranium-233, a fissile material that can be burned up as fuel in nuclear reactors. This is known as the Thorium-Uranium fuel cycle. When we reference Thorium reactors, this is the cycle that takes place within that reactor. The need to receive a neutron to turn Thorium into Uranium-233 is why the neutron economy of a reactor is essential. When running efficiently, with a good neutron economy, the reactor will "breed" its fuel by turning Thorium into Uranium. However, to start that cycle, you need a quantity of fissile material in your reactor, such as U-233, U-235 or Plutonium-239.

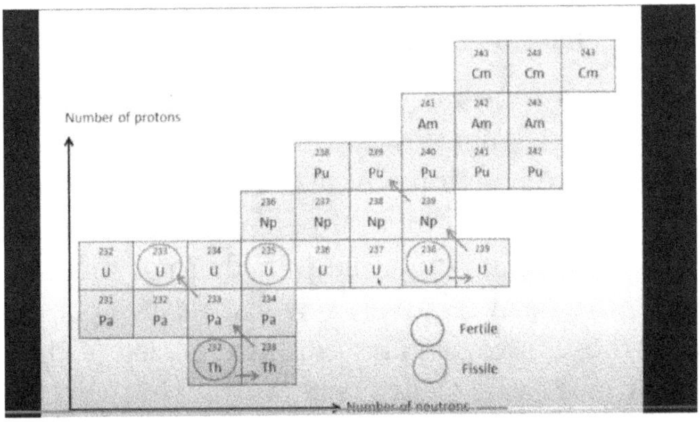

Figure 4.  Fertile and Fissile - decay routes

## Thermal and Fast Reactors

A thermal-neutron reactor uses slow or thermal neutrons. Most nuclear reactors are thermal and use a neutron moderator to slow neutrons and reduce their speed to low-velocity thermal neutrons. In some designs, water can be used as a coolant and moderator, but many moderators with different properties are possible.

The nuclear cross section of U-235 for slow thermal neutrons is about 1000 barns, while for fast neutrons, it is in the order of 1 barn. Therefore, thermal neutrons are more likely to cause U-235 to fission than to be captured by U-238 (to become U239). If at least one neutron from the U-235 fission strikes another nucleus and causes it to fission, then the chain reaction will continue. Thermal neutrons are more likely to be absorbed and transmuted by another heavy element, such as U-238, U-235, or Th-232. Only the U-235 has a high probability of fission.

In a fast (spectrum) reactor, high-energy (fast) neutrons with energies above 1 MeV sustain the fission chain reaction. A fast reactor needs no neutron moderator but requires fuel relatively rich in fissile material compared to a thermal reactor. There have been relatively few fast reactors built, and all those have been liquid metal cooled (either Sodium or Lead). Fast reactors provide certain advantages over water-cooled and water-moderated reactors. More neutrons are produced when fission occurs in a fast reactor than in a comparable process with thermally moderated neutrons. Thus, criticality is easier to attain than with slower neutrons.

Most moderated reactors use low-enriched fuel (processed to raise the concentration of U235). After 12–18 months of stable operation in moderated reactors, the reactor consumes more fissionable material than it breeds and accumulates neutron-absorbing fission products (like Plutonium-240 and heavier elements), making it difficult to sustain the fission process. When too much fuel has been consumed, the reactor has to be refuelled. Atoms heavier than uranium have a much greater chance of fission with a fast neutron than a thermal one. This means that the inventory of heavier atoms in the fuel is greatly reduced, leading to a substantially lower refuelling and waste management requirement. More of the fuel and potential waste is burnt in fast reactors, which are more efficient in this regard.

## Breeder, Converter and Burner Reactors

These terms refer to the fuel cycle used in the reactor. Most commercial reactors up to this point have been converter-type reactors. PWR, boiling water reactors and gas-cooled reactors are typically of this type [23]. They are fueled, the reaction is started, and the fuel is used until it becomes too contaminated by other actinides and noble gases to be used further. These reactors mainly use enriched uranium fuel rods. Most of the high-level waste from these reactors is used fuel rods. In this type of reactor, only a tiny proportion of the fuel has been entirely burned before they become unusable. The fuel can be reprocessed to recycle the unused fuel and separate the contaminates, but this is necessarily expensive and produces materials that are high risk in terms of proliferation.

Breeder reactors make the fuel for the fission chain reaction through the Thorium-Uranium or Uranium-Plutonium fuel cycle. In this process, excess neutrons are absorbed by the fertile material and converted into fissile material. It is possible to make breeder reactors so efficient that they never need refuelling (fed only with fertile material). They can even create the fissile material to start further reactors.

A key point to note about breeder reactors is that they do not reach a positive breeding balance overnight where they are creating as much (or more) fuel as is being consumed and where you only have to add fertile material. You may have to add fresh fuel for several years before you have converted sufficient amounts of fertile material to be self-sustaining. This depends on the fuel mix.

Lastly, burner reactors are designed to consume existing nuclear waste, either old uranium fuel rods and/or plutonium. In this process, these reactors may also create new fissile material, thus becoming a hybrid breeder-burner reactor that can potentially run on many fuel types.

# Chapter 4 Molten Salt Reactors

This chapter will concern itself with the advantages and major design considerations for the most promising types of molten salt reactors. Subsequent chapters will consider some of the technical and political issues that still need to be addressed, as well as the current state of the technology and industrial base (that is, readiness to build a commercial reactor).

We will be concentrating on reactors that use fuel in liquid form. In these, the molten salt contains the fuel and is also used to cool the reactor. There are also types of reactors that use solid fuel with liquid salt only used for cooling. However, this negates some of the advantages because the reactor has to be stopped to refuel it, and the levels of waste are higher.

Another advantage of liquid salt is it is easy to separate and remove elements that we don't want to be there. Keeping the liquid salts free of the by-products of the fission process is essential to smooth operations and managing the corrosion that could otherwise be a problem with liquid salt. The metallurgy involved in this is proven and well-understood after much research. All (nuclear) fission reactions produce various by-products like the noble gasses xenon and argon, tritium, and actinides. In a conventional solid fuel reactor, these are often trapped in the fuel and cause the fuel to be contaminated. Thus, there is a need for it to be replaced before it is fully used up, which is problematic or unwanted because it cannot easily be separated from solid fuel. These by-products have been used to argue against LFTR [6] when the opposite is true. In an MSR, these can be separated and sold as valuable products in their own right. Xenon and Argon have many industrial uses, and tritium is used in night vision equipment. Actinides are rare and only produced in small quantities by the reactor process, but they have valuable applications, especially in medicine for cancer treatment.   This part of the process deserves further discussion as these by-products are often cited about nuclear proliferation concerns, so that we will return to it in Chapter 6.

All historical and recent concepts rely either on fluoride or chloride salts. Other halides or other salts (e.g. the industrially utilised nitrate salt) are not considered because one or more of their properties, such as radiolysis of the salt without recombination, high neutron absorption or activation, low solubility of fuel salt or unfavourable melting points, disqualify them for use in the reactor core.

If spent fuel is not reprocessed, the fuel cycle is referred to as an 'open' or 'once-through' fuel cycle; if spent fuel is reprocessed and partly reused, it is referred to as a 'closed' nuclear fuel cycle.

The latest taxonomy produced by the IAEA divides MSRs into three major classes (and one minor) according to the type of materials present in the core. Graphite is the sole moderator directly compatible with the salt, so it plays a dominant role in the taxonomy. I don't intend to go into detail about the taxonomy, as we can just concentrate on the most relevant MSR.

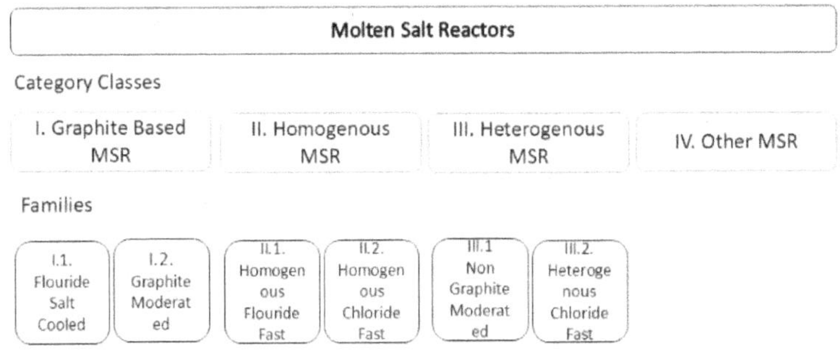


Figure 5. Taxonomy of Molten Salt Reactors [25]

## Class I: Graphite-based MSRs

These are characterised by the presence of graphite in the core and employ exclusively fluoride salt and a thermal spectrum. Since the graphite is directly compatible with the salt, no other structural material is needed in the core. This class has the highest technology readiness level because of the successful operation of the MSRE and because of some concepts' similarity to high-temperature reactors.

## Class II: Homogeneous MSRs

These are characterised by the absence of structural materials in the core that separate the fuel salt from a coolant or a moderator. The core is thus filled solely by the fuel salt. Optionally, structural materials (e.g. baffles for flow direction) can be present in the core; however, they do not have the separation function. The technology readiness level of this class depends mainly on the fuel salt, and for some of the MSRs using similar salts to those of the MSRE or the MSBR, the technology readiness level can be higher than others.

## Class III: Heterogeneous MSRs

These are characterised by structural materials in the core that separate the fuel salt from a dedicated coolant or a moderator not directly compatible with the fuel salt. The technology readiness level of this class also depends on the separation material, and it can be lower than for the previous two classes because these materials still need to be qualified.

## Class IV: Other MSRs

These do not fit into the three major classes and generally have the lowest technology readiness level.

## Advantages of Molten Salt reactors

Almost all the advantages of MSR can be broadly categorised in two ways: safety or economics. MSRs also have advantages regarding the environment and non-proliferation of nuclear material [24].

## Safety Advantages

### Near Atmospheric Operating Pressure

A salt circuit and confinement at ambient pressure removes the possibility of an "explosion" caused by the failure of structural materials under pressure. The risk of radioactive nuclide dispersion outside the containment is eliminated.

### Radioisotope Retention

Due to the chemical and thermophysical properties of molten salts, which bond strongly with many fission products even at high temperatures, this becomes an additional impediment to releasing radionuclides and is an intrinsic safety feature of MSR. Conversely, water-cooled reactors generate a much more comprehensive range of unretained fission products. These accumulate in the fuel rods and are highly volatile, creating the primary source of contamination in the event of an accident.

### Chemically inert and non-flammable

Molten salts have low chemical reactivity with either air or water, and there is no potential for hydrogen explosions or sodium fires. The containment of radioisotopes is more straightforward than in reactors using high-pressure fluids (water or helium) or reactive fluids like sodium.

## Removal of Gaseous Fission Products (FP)

Gaseous FP (i.e. Noble gasses) can be removed by separating them from the fuel salt during reactor operation, thus avoiding pressure build-up in the core. This mitigates the risk around the reactor compartment and the consequences of accident scenarios involving the core.

## No irradiation damage or mechanical failure of the fuel

Molten salt is an ionic liquid, and irradiation damage or mechanical failure cannot occur.

## Strong Negative Reactivity Temperature Feedback

This means that as the temperature in the core rises, the fuel salt reacts to resist this rise and lowers the temperature. This is due to fuel salt expansion reducing the density of fissionable material and the Doppler effect. The fuel moderator (e.g. graphite) can also have a role. This characteristic provides intrinsic stability for the core and enables passive shutdown for any temperature rise. It enhances safety and provides other benefits such as load following (that is, it is easy to raise or reduce the reactor's power output according to the grid's needs). Both Fast and Thermal spectra molten salt reactors benefit from this feature.

## Molten Salt as a Heat sink

After a reactor shutdown, the molten salt absorbs some decay heat. Moderated cores have even more capability in this regard due to the extra mass provided by the moderator. In fast and thermal MSR with fuel salt, thermal inertia is higher than that of equivalent solid fuel designs. MSR designs offer a simple way to dissipate heat by circulating the fuel through a heat exchanger. This design also eliminates the need for a separate cooling liquid to circulate the core, reducing the complexity of design and construction and potential points of failure.

## High boiling point

Molten salts have very high boiling points, which, in combination with the heat capacity of the salts, allows a considerable margin, up to 700 C, between the normal operating temperature and the boiling point.   This gives a great deal of headroom to operate the reactor in normal or abnormal scenarios without losing the cooling capability of the salt.

## Excellent Neutron Economy

MSR technology allows full utilisation of fuel loaded in the reactor core compared to solid fuel reactors. In conventional reactors, only a tiny proportion of the fuel is fissioned before reprocessing. In an MSR, 99% of all the fuel will be consumed, which reduces the amount of waste and significantly improves the amount of electricity generated from a given amount of fuel. The realisable energy density of the fuel in an MSR is many times higher. This is because of the absence of metallic structures, burnable poisons and other elements that will capture (and waste) neutrons.

Adding periodic fission product removal processes can improve the neutron economy, allowing break-even or breeding operations.

## Flexible Fuel Cycle

A reactor with liquid fuel can host all the actinide elements within the core and enable their continuous recycling, even those producing intense decay heat. Conversely, the solid fuel cannot be adjusted following manufacture and is vulnerable to mechanical and radiation damage and requires periodic replacement.

The flexibility of the liquid fuel cycle supports the breeding of fissile isotopes by using Th-232 or U-238 and recycling existing waste and other transuranic elements. This is a major advantage from an environmental and non-proliferation perspective [24]. Furthermore, if recycling is performed within the core or on-site, the risks related to spent fuel transportation are reduced or eliminated.

## Economic Advantages

The intrinsic safety of MSRs naturally has a positive knock-on effect on the economics and costs of building and running such a plant. The following features contribute to these advantages:

## High Temperature

MSRs have higher thermodynamic efficiency because they operate at higher temperatures, typically over 600 degrees centigrade. This generates steam through a heat exchanger more effectively than PWR operating at lower temperatures (Rankine cycle). Water-cooled technology is limited to around 300 degrees. It also offers the possibility of using gas (e.g. $CO_2$) driven turbines for high pressure followed by a lower pressure conventional steam turbine (Brayton cycle). This resembles a combined cycle gas-fired power plant (CCGT). $CO_2$ Brayton cycle technology offers the possibility of a much smaller turbine, which results in some obvious cost advantages.

Additionally, the high operating temperatures can support some industrial processes that require higher temperatures. A large market exists for output temperatures in the 550C range that MSRs can produce. Ammonia is used for liquid fuel production and fertiliser, petrochemical processes, aluminium smelting, and desalination plants, to name a few potential processes.

## Effective load following

MSRs provide excellent operational flexibility due to their ability to regulate their output easily. This is due to the negative temperature coefficient of the molten salt fuel. The negative feedback reactivity happens very quickly when the heat is produced directly in the coolant while the fuel salt is also in the coolant. This enables them to respond rapidly to the grid's needs to raise or lower electrical output - precisely the opposite of wind /solar that cannot load follow. As soon as the salt temperature varies because the power (heat) extracted has changed, the near-instantaneous variation of the salt density modifies the power generated. This is because removing power makes the salt more dense. When it becomes denser, the nuclear reaction intensifies due to the higher density of fissionable products, and the inverse is also true.

"This property fits well with an energy grid whose energy mix gives a larger share to intermittent sources" [24]

In practice, the ramp-up rates will not be because of the reactor physics but because of the limitations of the turbine technologies. MSR have considerable advantages over water-cooled, solid-fuel reactors because liquid fuel allows Xenon gases to be passively filtered out, avoiding the Xenon poisoning that occurs in conventional reactors. Those familiar with events leading to the Chornobyl disaster will appreciate the role played by the difficulties in varying the reactor output, including Xenon poisoning.

## High Resource Utilisation

The utilisation of fuel resources in an MSR is considerably higher than in solid fuel reactors. A strong neutron economy, radiation stability of the carrier salt, and the ability to continuously remove fission by-products and adjust the fuel composition allow for higher burnup, lower initial fissile fuel enrichment, and lower waste. Breeders or burners can utilise all the actinides from the spent fuel of existing reactors.

MSRs will burn over 99% of the reactor's fuel (and actinides) compared to sub 5% fuel burnup in solid fuel reactors. This provides 9,000 MWH / kg energy for a Th232-U233 (thermal reactor) and U238-PU239 (fast reactor) fuel cycles.

## Fuel Qualification - regulatory approval

The regulatory approval process for any solid fuel design takes years of testing to ensure the integrity of the fuel and the fuel cladding. This process is much more straightforward for liquid fuels, and much of the research and work has already been completed. The fuel composition and thermophysical changes can be done by modelling across the MSR lifetime without requiring extensive and time-consuming irradiation programmes, as the salts are not damaged and do not suffer radiolytic decomposition. [24]

## Compact Form Factor

Liquid fuel designs allow for optimal utilisation of the reactor core volume; that is, they are smaller than conventional reactors. Using liquid fuel for thermal spectrum reactors allows modularity in the design and the possibility of decentralised nuclear power production.

## Liquid Flouride Thorium Reactor - LFTR

"[A] LFTR may consume about 99% of its thorium fuel. The improved fuel efficiency means that one metric ton of natural thorium in an LFTR produces as much energy as 35t of enriched uranium in conventional reactors (requiring 250t of naturally mined uranium) or 4,166,000 tons of black coal in a coal power plant." [source]

This reactor comes from a class I, 2nd family of our taxonomy: Graphite moderated - two fluid Th-U breeder. This reactor has the following key characteristics.

- It is a thermal spectrum reactor.

- It uses a Thorium - Protactinium - Uranium 233  breeding fuel cycle

- An alternative burner fuel cycle uses enriched Uranium or Plutonium, which can be used for the initial load of the reactor to start the conditions for Th-U breeding.

- It is graphite moderated in the core (i.e. the graphite is in direct contact with the fuel salt). In addition to its ability to withstand neutron irradiation, Graphite offers impermeability to fuel salt and fission product gasses. Graphite is also used as a neutron reflector surrounding the core/blanket.

- It uses fluoride-based salt to carry fissionable fuel (usually U233) and act as a coolant.

- It has an outer layer (separate from the core) called a blanket layer that wraps the core. This is chemically similar to fluoride molten salt containing Thorium and helps protect the heat exchangers and reactor structures.

- The fluoride salt is colloquially known as FLiBe and contains highly depleted Li7 and Beryllium; it also has a relatively low melting point (456 degrees C) and a high volumetric heat capacity.   (7LiF-Be-F4 or as the fuel salt 7LiF-BeF2-233UF4)

- Prismatic graphite structures comprise most of the core volume, enabling a neutronically efficient design. The fuel salt and the blanket salt are carried by graphite tubes in the core. Graphite reflectors protect the reactor walls.

- All primary structures in the reactor are made from Hastelloy-N, a nickel alloy.

- Two reactor vessels are used in the design so that fuel can be pumped from one to the other to allow for the maintenance of the graphite core.

- Fission product gasses are held in a shielded cell until they form stable isotopes (about one month) and can then be separated and utilised (sold).

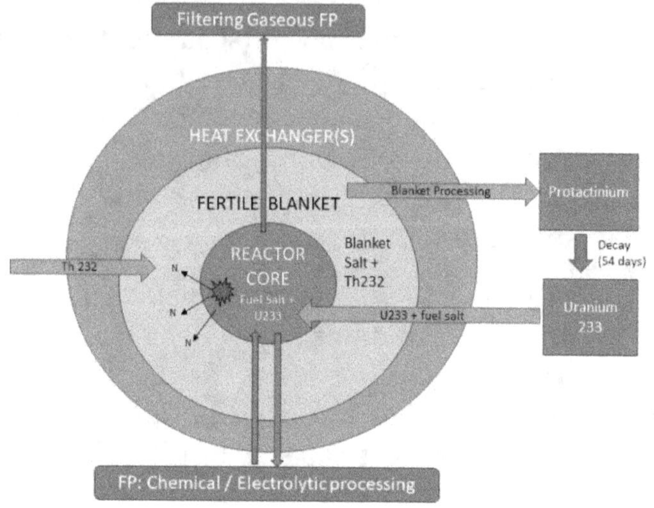


Figure 6.   LFTR Fuel Cycle

## LFTR Operations

Once the reactor core is initially fueled with fission products, thorium (TH232) is dissolved into the blanket salt and introduced to the blanket layer. In the blanket layer, the Th232 is bombarded with neutrons from the core, which it absorbs, thus becoming Protactinium (Pa-233).

Pa-233 must be regularly and rapidly removed from the blanket salt layer as it will absorb further neutrons (thus damaging the neutron economy and breeding of the reactor). The PA-233 can be chemically removed from the blanket salt and stored. Pa-233 has a very short half-life of c. 27 days and decays to U233, which is highly fissile. It is kept separate from the reactor until sufficient concentration has become U233. The U233 is pumped into the reactor core and carried in fuel salt.

Fission product gases (e.g. Xenon, Argon, etc) are filtered out continuously (existing boiled water reactors also have gaseous filtration).   Other fission products can be filtered periodically using a discriminator where voltage controls the electrolytic process.   Those actinides we don't want (to extract) can be left in the fuel salt to be burned in the reactor.

There is an intermediate heat exchanger surrounding the reactor containing the same fluoride-based salt as the reactor; this is there to provide an additional trap for any residual neutrons and tritium that we don't want to get into our gas heat exchanger. This protects the high-pressure gas heat exchanger from the neutron flux so that it has greater longevity. The gas heat exchanger takes the reactor heat off to the turbines via $CO_2$ gas. Excess heat can be recovered and pass through another low-pressure heat exchanger to make steam power a second turbine. Once the energy has passed to/through the gas heat exchanger, the design considerations for electricity generation are mostly the same as for conventional gas-fired power stations.

In addition to the naturally moderating effects of the fuel salt, the reactor can be passively stopped whenever the temperature climbs above a safety threshold or for any other reason. The reactor fuel salt can be drained by gravity into a storage tank beneath the reactor. Once the fuel salt is removed from the graphite moderator in the core, the fission reaction cannot continue.  A salt plug sits at the bottom of the reactor, and it will melt if it becomes too hot (it has a known melting point). Another way to achieve this is to require the fuel salt to be continuously and actively pumped into the reactor. If the pump stops, the fuel drains out of the reactor and into the storage tank.

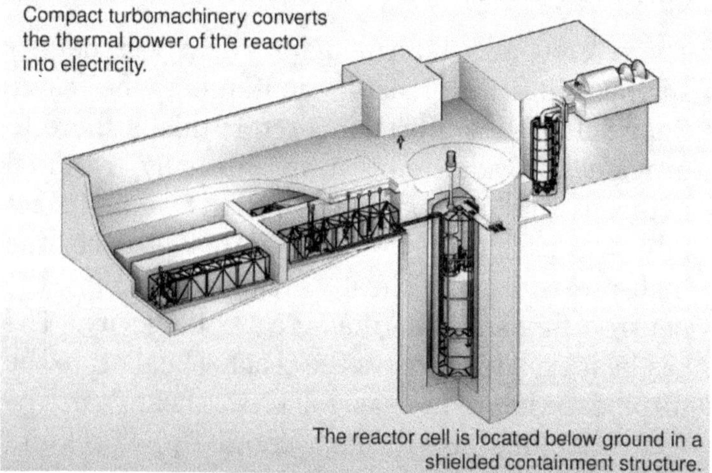


*Figure 7. LFTR Facility Concept. Copyright Kirk Sorenson, FLiBE Energy.*

Note that the treatment plants for the blanket salt and the fuel salts sits on the left, and the generation machinery on the right of the diagram. The reactor cell sits in the ground to give physical protection from outside threats (e.g. aircraft strikes).

## LFTR Advantages

In addition to the generic advantages already mentioned concerning MSR Liquid Flouride Thorium Reactors of this design have the following additional benefits.

Fundamental elements have already been demonstrated and proven, including the role of graphite. This type of reactor was run at the Oak Ridge National Laboratory in the USA during the 1960s-70s, so the Experiments were carried out on the critical structural materials for safety and longevity, and further experimental work has been done on these over the past decade or so.

FLiBE salts have good heat transfer properties between 500 - 700 degrees C. This gives the reactor an excellent operating range. FLiBE salts also have a relatively low melting temperature and are neutronically compatible with Graphite, Thorium, and Uranium in the fuel salt.  Unlike Light Water reactors, all the major components are in equilibrium. The cost of FLiBe salts is relatively insignificant in terms of the operating costs of an LFTR.

Using graphite as a moderator reduces the amount of fissile material needed to load the reactor fuel salt initially.  It also protects the reactor vessel and components. The individual graphite rods within the core can be inspected by the camera and replaced if any have been damaged. This protects the separation of the fuel salt from the fertile salt.  Thermal rather than fast reactivity also reduces the speed of irradiation within the graphite, prolonging its lifespan.

LFTR thermal reactors have an excellent neutron economy with 2.3 net neutrons produced in the core. This allows for very successful fuel breeding and flexible operation.

When considering the TH-U fuel cycle, it should be noted that the U233, as used in an LFTR, is worthless for all practical purposes as a weapon due to contamination with U232. This was the reason it was rejected early in the US weapons programme.  There are no designs and no knowledge of weapons using U233, making it completely impractical to use for any sub-nation-sized bad actor. Any nation-sized state would use more accessible routes containing Plutonium or enriched Uranium 235; there is no reason for them to go the troublesome route of trying to use U233.

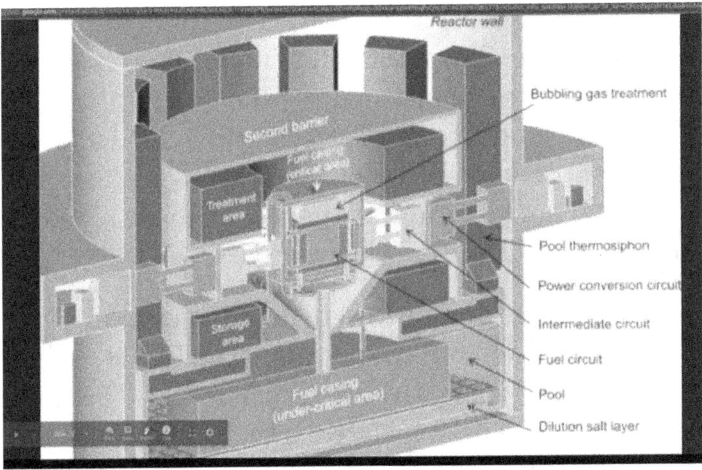


*Figure 8. LFTR*

## LFTR Disadvantages

Reactors that use FLiBe salts will produce Tritium due to the neutron activation of the Lithium and Beryllium. Tritium production (H3), along with other activation reactions on FLiBe, is an oxidising process that leads to the corrosion of salt-facing metallic components in the absence of redox control [26]. In addition to tritium production as an oxidising process, Li breeding from Be and O breeding from F also make non-negligible contributions to the oxidising effects of neutron irradiation in FLiBe.

The consequence of oxidising activation reactions is that electrons must be consumed from components dissolved in or in contact with the salt (i.e., oxidising reactions must occur). When the oxidised elements are metals from salt-facing metallic components, corrosion occurs. This impact is that corrosion levels of 4 microns per year must be allowed for in some of the pipework and structural components (The reactor core is shielded from direct contact with the salts by graphite). Secondly, it is important that the chemical composition of the salt is maintained at the same level and free from impurities.

We need large amounts of highly depleted Lithium (i.e. with Li6 removed) for the FLiBe salts. Lithium 6 negatively affects the neutron economy, breeds unwanted tritium and increases corrosion through oxidation.

The graphite tubes in the core require regular inspection and maintenance. For this reason, a certain level of redundancy is required in reactor vessels, which is why two vessels are proposed.

At the end of the reactor's life, after about 50 to 60 years, the graphite used in the core will be irradiated and disposed of as waste. To put this into context, 90% of the waste produced by a solid fuel reactor over its lifetime is the used fuel rods. LFTR does not have waste fuel; the remaining 10% is the reactor and moderator.

Reactors like the Advanced Gas Cooled and MAGNOX reactors used in the UK were all graphite-moderated, and these are being decommissioned, which has created a considerable quantity of waste that is currently being or about to be disposed of. Methods previously involved this being left for several years to 'cool' before being sent to a repository.

However, new methods could involve gasification. Oxidising the graphite by heating it with air turns it into carbon monoxide or carbon dioxide. Separating the irradiated C14 elements from the rest of the material as gas or via other processes may be possible.

Using two fluid designs creates complexity because an additional circuit for the fuel blanket is required. This is balanced by having the protective effect of the blanket and more stable operating scenarios for the fuel salt. There are also some neutronic advantages to separating the two.

## LFTR Wasteburner - Copenhagen Atomics

This design is from the class of Heterogeneous MSRs (III), in the family of non-graphite moderated MSRs (III.5). This design is another LFTR but with some key differences: it is a single-fluid, heavy water moderated, fluoride-based, and thermal spectrum molten salt reactor, developed by Copenhagen Atomics. It is highly modular and compact, designed to fit inside a leak-tight, 40-foot stainless steel shipping container. The heavy water moderator is thermally insulated from the salt, continuously drained, and cooled to below 50 °C (thus operating at atmospheric pressure). A molten lithium-7 deuteroxide (7LiOD) moderator version is also being researched. The reactor utilises the thorium fuel cycle while using separated plutonium from spent nuclear fuel as the initial fissile load for the first generation of reactors, eventually transitioning to a thorium breeder in a closed cycle.

This design removes some of the complexity of the two fluid designs and does away with the graphite, reducing solid waste. However, the heavy water would also become irradiated and would contain tritium (you can't separate tritium from water - but it is only a beta emitter, so it is not considered very dangerous in low quantities). Eventually, the irradiated heavy water would need to be disposed of. Recycling treats the water to remove strontium and radionuclides through filtration, distillation, and vaporisation. Filtering the water decontaminates it to a level suitable for release or use in other processes.

The salt used in this reactor is FLiNaK - Fluoride Lithium Sodium Potassium.

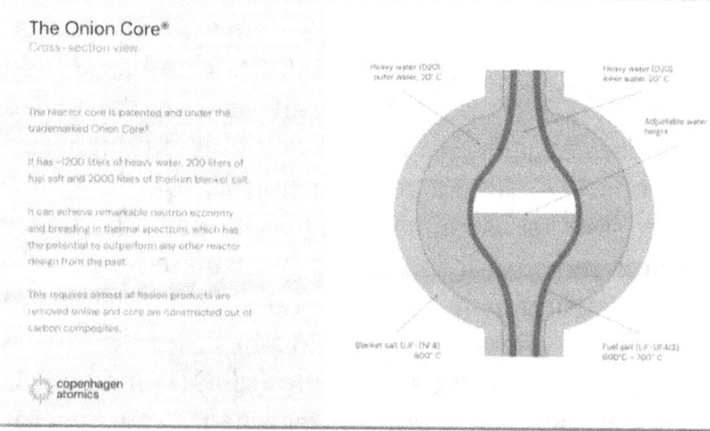


*Figure 9.    LFTR Wasteburner.    Copyright Copenhagen Atomics*

Safety is still passive, with the fuel draining away from the moderator to stop the reaction. There are thermal barriers between the fuel salt and the heavy water. In the event of these mixing and steam being created, this can be recovered back to water by cooling or venting within the local containment. Spillages of fuel salt would be managed within the containment.

The mechanical separation of fission products is achieved through vacuum spraying, where the salt leaving the core is sprayed into a chamber at a partial vacuum pressure, and the volatility of intermediate decay products is used to extract a large fraction of the fission products. The extracted fission products are separated and stored in tanks inside a leak-tight stainless steel containment. The start-up phase begins with the initial $LiF–ThF_4–PuF_4$ fuel composition. U233 production benefits from the high number of excess neutrons from the plutonium fission. Later, the breeding process benefits from the superior neutron economy of U233 as the fuel converges towards its equilibrium composition of $LiF–ThF_4–233UF_4$. Thus, the Copenhagen Atomics Waste Burner is expected to be a breeder reactor when the fuel has reached this composition.

Copenhagen Atomics have completed 2m hours of testing on some of the key components and controls, which is ongoing.

*Figure 11. Copenhagen Atomics - conceptual visualisation - 1GW plant*

## LFTR Wasteburner - disadvantages.

The life of this reactor is only 4 to 5 years. This is deliberate so that the whole container can simply be swapped for another reactor container and shipped out to be reprocessed. This also means that the components, such as the pumps, can be designed to run without any maintenance for the life of the reactor. Although this is a deliberate design decision and can be seen as advantageous, the expected movement of the reactor containers in and out of the facility and safety considerations will be the downside.

The use of heavy water as a moderator also has some drawbacks, for example:

- The high cost of heavy water to manufacture.

- Leakage is a potential problem as there are two mechanically sealed closures per fuel channel.

- High standards of design, manufacture inspection and maintenance are required.

Heavy water is used because it doesn't capture thermal neutrons. Graphite is somewhat better than light water; however, water also has the advantage of being a coolant. If coolant is lost, the fission process will shut down without the moderator being present.

## Homogeneous Molten Chloride Fast Reactor (MCSFR)

Elyssium Industries Inc. has produced the design for this reactor. The principal difference between this reactor and LFTR is using chloride salts instead of FLiBe; it operates in the fast spectrum due to the absence of light nuclei on the carrier salt and does not require any moderator (such as graphite) in the core. This feature means the reactor can operate as a breeder in either the U-Pu cycle or less frequently in the Th-U cycle. In the self-sustaining breed and burn U-Pu cycle, all the actinides are left in the fuel, which avoids the need for enrichment, reprocessing or separation (of the actinides).    Additionally, burner applications make it possible to simply consume waste from solid fuel reactors.

In the homogenous chloride fast MSR, the active core is composed of fuel salt with no structural material to affect the neutronics. The heat exchange occurs outside the active region, and the power is released directly into the fuel salt. The higher solubility of actinides in chloride salts allows for an increased density of actinides compared with fluoride salts.

Due to the hard spectrum that results from chloride salts, a reflector layer is needed to counter the relatively transparent neutron path. From a thermohydraulic perspective, the chloride salts share similar characteristics with fluoride salts, having good heat transfer properties and showing slight differences in heat capacity, density and viscosity. The chloride salts have a slightly lower melting point than fluoride salts.

The use of chloride salts is less mature than fluoride salts, which means that further work is needed to ensure the capability of structural materials with chloride salts and their performance against corrosion. Silicon carbide has a significantly larger resistance to reactor irradiation than fuel salt-compatible metal alloys.
This reactor has been designed to work with Sodium Chloride (NA-Cl) as the base salt. It uses a Cl-37 isotope at 70-95% concentration, which is non-weapons grade from a proliferation/risk perspective.

These reactors could be built with standard stainless steel reactor vessels, currently licensed for use in nuclear reactors. However, this would limit the operating temperature to less than 700 degrees Celsius. The use of more advanced alloys would allow the temperature to be raised.

If burning waste nuclear fuel and Plutonium (90%/10%) mix, it should be noted that all the nuclear material is denatured (not weapons grade) and contained within the reactor and fuel salts at all times during the operations.  This means that it is impossible to remove it as it is radioactively hot (with lots of short-lived isotopes) and chemically hot, plus it is mixed with fission products, thus effectively protecting it. Obviously, this is in addition to any physical security measures.

The reactor design has two-stage heat exchangers. The first (primary) heat exchanger contains liquid salt (the secondary salt is still sodium chloride), and the second is a superheater. The nature of this would depend on the requirements for generating power. However, this has the same design considerations as LFTR, gas-cooled reactors and closed-cycle natural gas thermal power plants.  Steam, hydrogen, nitrogen or $CO_2$ can be used in secondary and tertiary systems. However, it is important to note that 85% of the cost of a power station is in the power conversion elements (i.e. the heat exchangers and turbines), and this is where we need to concentrate on optimising the design. The reactor vessel and fuel circulation is only 15% of the total cost.

There is no reactor freeze plug.  Fuel is pumped up continuously from the supply/drain tank.  If the reactor is tripped (automatically shut down) due to either a high or low (danger of salt freezing) temperature trip, the fuel salt drains down once the pumps stop.

THE MOLTEN CHLORIDE SALT FAST REACTOR (MCSFR)

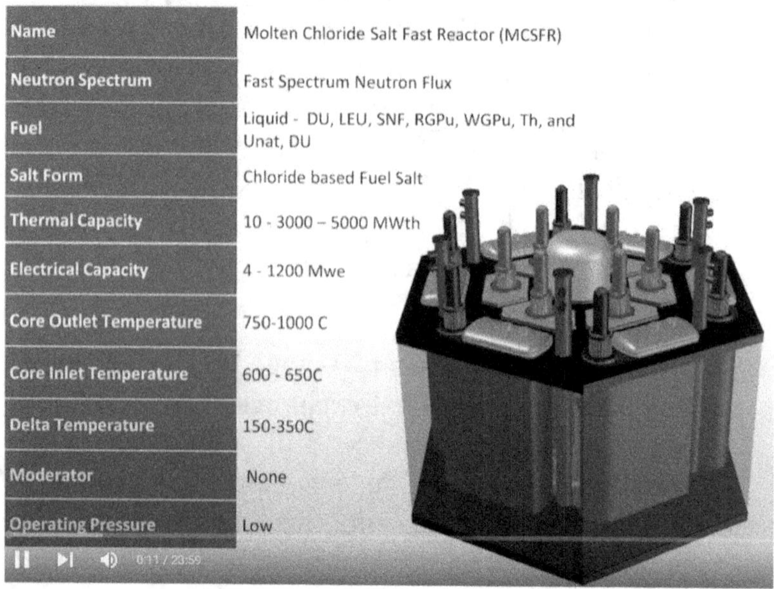

| Name | Molten Chloride Salt Fast Reactor (MCSFR) |
| --- | --- |
| Neutron Spectrum | Fast Spectrum Neutron Flux |
| Fuel | Liquid - DU, LEU, SNF, RGPu, WGPu, Th, and Unat, DU |
| Salt Form | Chloride based Fuel Salt |
| Thermal Capacity | 10 - 3000 – 5000 MWth |
| Electrical Capacity | 4 - 1200 Mwe |
| Core Outlet Temperature | 750-1000 C |
| Core Inlet Temperature | 600 - 650C |
| Delta Temperature | 150-350C |
| Moderator | None |
| Operating Pressure | Low |



*Figure 11 MCSFR - copyright Elysium Industries.*

## Advantages of MCSFR

The main advantage of an MCSFR is that it can burn many types of fuel. Stocks of plutonium and waste uranium fuel rods can be chopped up and dissolved in the liquid chloride salt in an open cycle. Alternatively, it can run as a breeder in a closed cycle on either U-Pu or TH-U; this requires a larger reactor core.   A fuel blanket could improve' breeding' for the Th-U cycle.

When used as a burner, the MCSFR produces about 36 times more power from a given amount of uranium than a conventional reactor using solid fuel rods. These burn about 4% of the fissile material, whereas an MCSFR will burn over 96%. Given this level of productivity, the spent solid fuel currently in storage would provide our electrical energy needs for hundreds of years. Based on US quantities of spent nuclear fuel, if 20% of the power were nuclear, it would take 360 years to burn all the spent fuel without further uranium mining.

The next advantage is the lack of structural materials in the core - e.g. graphite fuel rods. This simplifies construction and maintenance but puts more strain on the reactor vessel, potentially reducing its life span. However, the reactor and any reflector cladding would now be the main consideration for lifespan rather than the graphite.

Owing to the reduced capture cross-section of the fission products in the fast spectrum, frequent salt treatment is unnecessary to remove neutron poisons. The actinides created in the fuel salt will be incinerated and allow for increased breeding possibilities, that is they provide additional free neutrons to convert fertile material to fissile. In a fast reactor, even U238 will provide power due to the higher speed neutrons, which create more free neutrons during collisions.

This reactor is designed to be modular in construction. The reactor vessel is a standard size due to the neutronics and to reduce construction costs by coming off a production line. The modularity comes from the ability to add or subtract key components like heat exchangers and pumps for the molten salt. These are mounted on the outside for ease of maintenance, and they are all independent of one another as there are no pipes connecting them, which minimises these construction elements. However, they all draw from a standard fuel supply/drain tank. Lastly, the fuel loop is relatively compact, cycling through the reactor and minimising the materials and costs. The intention is to mass produce the reactor vessels and ship them as complete or partially complete reactors to the site. There is potential for modular scale-up.

The reactor operates at the same or higher temperatures as high-temperature gas-cooled reactors (HTGR), like the advanced gas-cooled reactors in the UK fleet now nearing their end of life. However, the MCSFR operates at lower, near atmospheric pressure. It also has a lower flow rate, which means that for HTGR, the pumps would run at 10,000 r.p.m., which improves longevity. It also has a much lower cost of fuel (liquid vs. solid fuel).

Compared with liquid metal cooled reactors, it has the same low pressure, but there is no risk of Sodium fires or need for their associated safety systems, which saves the corresponding costs. It also runs at a higher temperature and efficiency, producing savings compared to solid fuel costs.

Chloride salts have a lower melting point than fluoride salts, so there is no need to add Lithium to lower the boiling point as we do with FLiBe. In turn, this means that you don't need to enrich Lithium to create a very pure Lithium-7, which makes FLiBe salts more expensive. Other advantages over LFTR reactors are even lower costs, assuming the use of waste fuel and plutonium. Furthermore, there is no graphite cost or materials in the core that can be damaged. Hence, operating costs will be lower because there is no graphite to change/renew every few years.

There is no need for chemical cleansing of the fuel salt; this is optional and depends on the desired operational life. Compared to the Copenhagen Atomics design, there is a reduced risk of water mixing with the fuel salt. Lastly, this design does not use a frozen salt plug to stop the reactor draining, which has to be cooled - thus saving this complexity.

In the MCSFR, there is no separation of proliferation-sensitive material during the reactor operation. These are all mixed in the fuel salts, where short-lived and highly radioactive fission products will protect the other elements. Of course, the fuel salt temperature is also hot, requiring special handling to remove from the reactor.

Finally, at the practical level, more chemists have worked with and are familiar with chloride salts than the more esoteric fluoride salts.

## Disadvantages of MCSFR

As with anything new in the nuclear industry, the regulatory approval hurdles are arduous and time-consuming, even in the best case. Getting approval for new types of solid fuel is complex, but the regulators are relatively well understood. However, the regulators have no experience with liquid fuel salts and, therefore, don't have any processes. This means that the fuel qualification cycle for Chloride salts will probably take several years, as will approval for the reactor design. The same issue occurs for the LFTR reactors, which are further down the design and testing cycle. In the case of the FLiBe reactor, the work done by the Oak Ridge National Laboratory forms a solid body of evidence and precedent.

Each reactor will need approximately 70 tonnes of spent fuel (SNF) to start, comprising 90% SNF and 10% weapons-grade plutonium (WGPu), assuming a 1 GWe reactor core. From this point, 10% of the reactor's power will come from 'breeding' U238 into fissile material. This is not a disadvantage to MCSFR because all the reactors must be initially fuelled with fissile material. However, it is relatively bulky because much of the SNF is other things like U238.

Although an MCSFR produces less waste over its life compared with a graphite-moderated reactor, you must still have plans to deal with the fission gases, cladding and insoluble fission products (e.g.

noble metals, and possibly Lanthanides).    If separated into their constituents, the fission gases (e.g. Krypton, Xenon and Radon) and many solid fission products are valuable materials that could be sold for other commercial uses.

At the end of the reactor's life (at least 40 years, depending on the operations), the reactor can be left to "cool". At this point, the fuel salts will contain sufficient fission products to start two more reactors.  If the fuel is not sent to another reactor, it can simply be left in place for just seven years, after which most short-lived radioactive nuclides will decay to make the reactor safe to decommission.

In MSRs with fast spectra, higher power densities make in-core instrumentation impractical, increasing the burden on developing monitoring techniques.  In general, instrumentation to sample the salts' physicochemical and dynamic properties has already been developed for other applications but needs to be adapted for use in MSRs.

Issues related to chemistry, such as corrosion, compatibility with structural material and stability of chloride salts, require further investigation. From a thermohydraulic perspective, the chloride salts share similar characteristics with fluoride salts, having good heat transfer properties and showing slight differences in heat capacity, density and viscosity. The chloride salts show a slightly lower melting point than fluoride salts.

## Operating Processes for MCSFR

As one of the most important advantages of MCSFR is the burning of spent fuel and /or weapons-grade plutonium, it seems reasonable to look at how the fuel would be prepared. Especially as the SNF would have to be transported, the same would happen for the plutonium (which would have to be done at a grade 1 security facility), so a dedicated facility would likely be required. The UK has developed a facility for handling and creating solid fuel rods with enriched uranium. The used fuel would be chopped into 2cm lengths and then dissolved into the salt in a special vessel (a process pioneered in Japan). From this, the gaseous fission products (i.e. Kr, Xe, Rn) are removed and stored for a month to become stable elements. This leaves the noble metals as particulates as these are not soluble in the salt. These are simply filtered out (by a particulate filter). The fuel is now ready to be used in the reactor. This fuel process is much cheaper than mining/refining uranium, enriching it and creating very high-quality, precise tolerance solid fuel rods.

This reactor operates in a state where it is only just critical. As it is a fast breeder, the concentration of actinides in the fuel salt and, hence the temperature can be balanced by adding fresh salt to lower the concentration.

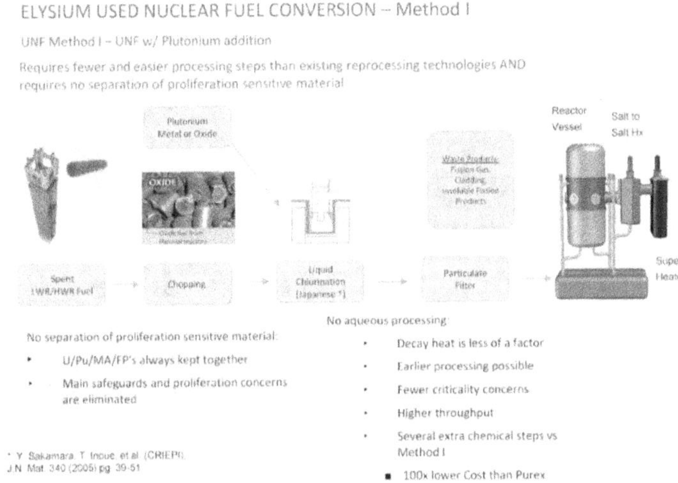



*Figure 12. Elysium Fuel Conversion Cycle (copyright Elysium Industries)*

During the reactor operation, the gases are removed on a continuous or 30-minute cycle. The particulates are filtered every 4 hours. However, no chemical processing is required if this is not desired. The soluble products lanthanides and actinides can be left in fuel salt until the end of the reactor life. This reduces the reactor life to about 40 years. If these products are removed (by chemical processing of the fuel salt), it could extend the reactor life up to 100 years (though this is unproven).

After the 40-year operating life, there will be sufficient amounts/ concentration of fissile material in the fuel salt to start two reactors.

During the reactor operation, it will consume about 3 kg /day (1 ton/year) of fuel (spent nuclear fuel) based on a 1 GW reactor. The heat exchangers are accessible from the top of the reactor, and the pumps are mounted on the heat exchangers. Heat exchangers and pumps can be swapped out/in for maintenance. All maintenance is done remotely via robots.

## Pebble Bed High-Temperature Gas Cooled Reactors (PBHTGR)

Most of the next (4th) generation designs are based on liquid fuel in molten salt (i.e. MSRs). Of course, the UK, being different, is opting for the High-Temperature Gas Cooled Reactors, a fast reactor that uses solid fuel pebbles, graphite moderator and helium for cooling.

The fuel comes in spherical pebbles coated in multiple layers of ceramics, making them highly resistant to melting, even in accident scenarios. The use of pebbles allows for continuous refuelling without shutting down the reactor. This results in less operational downtime and potentially higher overall capacity factors.

The passive cooling design of the PBHTGR allows it to shut down and cool without active intervention. Helium, the coolant used, is inert and does not become radioactive, which reduces the risk of chemical reactions, such as hydrogen production, that can lead to explosions (again, no water and limited pressure).

The reactor operates at high temperatures (up to 950°C), allowing for higher thermal efficiency than traditional reactors. This can lead to better energy conversion rates and potentially lower electricity costs. The high temperature can also be used in industrial processes, like hydrogen production, which expands the reactor's utility beyond electricity generation. Like other fast reactor designs, it will generate less high-level radioactive waste as it will better utilise the nuclear fuel, achieving higher burn-up rates.

PBHTGRs are often designed as modular reactors, meaning smaller units can be constructed and scaled according to demand. This can reduce upfront capital costs and make nuclear energy accessible to smaller grids.

PBHTGR designs are also compatible with thorium fuel cycles, which are more abundant and create less long-lived radioactive waste than uranium.

Some of the disadvantages of the design are the high costs of manufacturing the fuel, both compared to traditional fuel rods and molten salt. A dedicated facility is required to manufacture the pebbles, which involves coating the fuel particles with multiple layers of ceramics to ensure containment and heat resistance.

While PBHTGRs produce less overall waste, the waste generated is high-temperature spent pebbles, which require careful handling and disposal. The volume of used pebbles could still be substantial.

The initial construction costs for PBHTGRs can be high due to the complexity of the design and the need for advanced materials capable of handling extreme temperatures. While PBHTGR technology has been tested in small experimental reactors, large-scale commercial deployment must be achieved and proven. Regulatory frameworks and safety protocols are less well-developed than they are for traditional nuclear plants.

Graphite, used in the reactor core, has certain disadvantages, such as graphite dust generation, which can pose operational challenges, and the risk of graphite fires in extreme accident scenarios. However, such risks are significantly mitigated in modern designs. Last but not least, the graphite eventually becomes radioactive waste.

Despite its theoretical advantages, only a few PBHTGRs have been built and operated. Most commercial nuclear power plants use light-water reactors, meaning operational expertise, supply chains, and regulatory frameworks for PBHTGRs are still developing.

The Pebble Bed High-Temperature Gas Reactor offers several promising advantages, particularly regarding safety and efficiency. However, it faces technical and economic challenges, especially in fuel manufacturing, initial costs, and scalability. Overall, the development of this technology is less advanced than that of some MSR designs. The next chapter discusses the route forward commercial application and deployment at scale for MSR designs.

# Chapter 5 Bringing Molten Salt Reactors to Commercial Readiness

It is a commonly held belief that nuclear reactors are slow to build and expensive. It is understandable, as we regularly hear about Hinckley Point cost overruns and delays. Therefore, we will look at all the elements of economics and implementation in further chapters. However, in this chapter, I want to discuss how soon we could build a commercial version of these MSRs and look into some of the issues that need to be resolved with these 4th generation reactors.

## Current status of LFTR technology

The FLiBe version of the LFTR is based on a working prototype that ran for several years at the Oak Ridge National Laboratory (ORNL) in Tennessee, USA. There were three versions of MSRs, and the copious information and documentation generated from the mid-sixties to the mid-seventies is the basis for much of the preliminary work elsewhere. Ultimately, the experiment was shut down, and the next step, which would have been to build a commercial-scale reactor, was never taken. However, the second and third experimental LFTR reactors ran for several years. They provided significant experimental results that informed the design decisions for the next steps, especially regarding the use of materials.   This still needs to be improved to build a full-scale commercial reactor, as one would expect there were still a number of operational issues that still needed to be fully resolved in terms of proving the longevity and ability to operate continuously at high loads.

Currently, the Chinese (Shanghai Institute of Applied Physics - SINAP) has built and is operating a small 2 MW LFTR (known as TMSR-LF1) near the city of Wuwei, intending to scale and build out bigger versions of this reactor. Also known as the fluoride salt-cooled high-temperature reactor, construction started in 2018 and went into operation in 2022. The TMSR-LF1 will use fuel enriched to under 20% U-235, with a thorium inventory of about 50 kg and a conversion ratio of about 0.1. A fertile blanket of lithium-beryllium fluoride (FLiBe) with 99.95% Li-7 will be used, and fuel salt will be used as Uranium Tetrafluoride ($UF_4$).

FLiBe was chosen as the fuel salt for the test reactors. This salt generates tritium when irradiated by neutrons. Research was conducted on stripping tritium from the salt using a bubbling system, tritium separation from noble gases using cryogenics, tritium storage using alloys and continuous tritium monitoring to prevent an uncontrolled tritium release into the environment.

Experiments using surrogate gases such as hydrogen and deuterium were carried out to evaluate the performance of different techniques. Some experiments were carried out on a palladium–silver alloy membrane diffuser, tritium storage alloy bed and oxidation post-treatment bed using hydrogen isotopes to simulate tritium control performance.

The project is expected to start on a batch basis with some online refuelling and removal of gaseous fission products but discharging all fuel salt after 5-8 years for reprocessing and separating fission products and minor actinides for storage. It will continue to recycle salt, uranium and thorium, with online separation of fission products and minor actinides. The reactor will work from about 20% thorium fission to 80%.

Verification activities include (i) the verification of fundamental principles, such as neutronic characteristics, thermohydraulic characteristics and reactor safety characteristics, and (ii) technical verification, such as verifying equipment and technology related to materials, fuel salt, molten salt, radiochemistry and loop and instrument and control systems. If the TMSR-LF1 proves successful, China plans to build a reactor with a capacity of 373 MWt by 2030. As this type of reactor does not require water for cooling, it can operate in desert regions.

In Japan, the FUJI MSR is a 100 - 1000 MW(e) design, graphite-moderated TH-U cycle reactor with high thermal efficiency (44%). It is designed to be compact and modular. FUJI can consume plutonium as the fissile material and can contribute to reducing the proliferation risk caused by plutonium from light water reactor spent fuel. It can also be used to transmute long lived minor actinides to shorter ones.

FUJI has very favourable safety characteristics that exclude the possibility of severe accidents. It is expected that FUJI can be deployed in less than ten years. FUJI is based on the results obtained by ORNL in the 1960s. It has been optimised as a small-sized plant and further simplified by removing the online reprocessing facility. Based on the experience of operating the three experimental MSRs at ORNL, it has been verified that FUJI is feasible. Three experimental reactors have been built, and detailed design work has started on a 200 MW version. The steam generator is a major unverified component, but it could be developed based on experience from the fast breeder reactor and the recent supercritical power station technology.

Each reactor design will have its pros and cons. However, once the fundamental decisions have been taken around the design and the moderator, the key elements that need to be refined are specifically around the design of the pumps and heat exchangers, the operating procedures around how to manage/separate the fusion products and how to manage the fuel cycle in detail.

# Copenhagen Atomics LFTR Wasteburner

The Copenhagen Atomics Wasteburner reactor is still in the conceptual and testing phases. Nuclear fission has yet to be attempted. The company is currently negotiating with various governments to site an initial reactor. The most advanced discussions are with Indonesia.

Much of the development work required for any power plant is the software that will run and oversee the different elements of the reactor and power generation systems. This can be written and tested independently of the reactor's build and critical components. Copenhagen Atomics has completed ten years of development for its control systems.

While many elements of reactor design can be modelled, simulated and proved using computer software, you can only demonstrate the longevity and reliability of all the elements of a reactor if you run them under realistic conditions for many years. Like all engineering designs, these things will be refined and improved over the years by making minor incremental improvements.

Copenhagen Atomics and its LFTR (using heavy water as a moderator) have built and tested the critical components of the fuel salt circulation systems and other elements for several years. They have also been progressing with the other aspects of the design, including the containers. Elements of this technology have been made available to universities in the UK and elsewhere for verification and other experiments.

Active development focuses on testing and validating materials, flanges, valves, pumps, heat exchangers, salt purification, chemistry control systems, measurement and autonomous control systems. All components are designed to last for the reactor's lifetime (5–10 years) without any service; for example, this is achieved for the pumps by using active electromagnetic bearings and a canned pump design. [26?]

Copenhagen Atomics is actively developing components considered to be state of the art for MSRs, including a canned rotor molten salt pump with electromagnetic bearings, molten salt valves, molten salt filters, molten salt flowmeters, qualification of commercial heat exchangers for use in MSRs, salt spraying off-gas systems, qualification of composite materials as salt wetted structural material in MSRs, fluoride salt purification, on-line molten salt redox metre, on-line laser breakdown spectroscopy metre, autonomous reactor control systems and software.

Copenhagen Atomics' objective is to have assembly line production of molten salt test loops and MSRs that are the size of a shipping container. Some of these research activities are carried out with university and industry partners.

## Molten Salt Fast Reactors - Current State

As we discussed before, one of the principle differences with fast reactors is that no moderator is required. The neutron moderation from fluoride salts is relatively high, so they cannot be used in reactors using a depleted U-Pu cycle, creating a need for a switch to chloride salts.

Using chloride salt was one of the first options considered during the first phase of developing MSR concepts. The use of salts based on fluoride was more favourable than chloride salts. The problem with chloride salts is the activation of $^{35}Cl$ into $^{36}Cl$, a long-lived isotope and a 0.7 MeV beta emitter. A solution to this radiotoxicity issue is the chlorine isotopic separation with enrichment in $^{37}Cl$, but this technology was not considered mature then. As a result, R&D efforts concentrated on fluoride carriers, limiting experimental data on chloride. In the 1950s, different concepts that involved chloride use in fast MSR were proposed.

The neutron flux in fast-spectrum MSRs can be significantly more extensive. Unless sufficient secondary salt shielding is inherent in the design, neutron-absorbing materials may also have to be included in the coating or cladding of the reactor vessels. For the same reason, unless novel, more radiation-resistant materials can be developed, the operational lifetimes of reactor internals in fast-spectrum MSRs will be short, necessitating frequent replacement and maintenance.

The EU Joint Research Centre (JRC) commenced investigating MSR in 2004 following a Generation IV International Forum selection process. This started with theoretical and experimental chemical research into molten salt fuel and fuel cycles. The extensive literature provided by the ORNL provided a base from which to start the research to improve the reliability of the models. The JRC in Karlsruhe now has a collection of instruments and facilities suitable for investigating molten salt fuels and a database of thermodynamic results from various fuels and coolants, including fluoride and chloride salts. The ongoing work has evolved into irradiation experiments in the High Flux Reactor and ensuring that fuels with appropriate purity are available for experimentation.

EU efforts have continued through several projects run under the Euratom programme. In the current Molten Salt Fast Reactor (MSFR - representative of a reactor with molten salt as fuel and coolant) design option, the blanket salt flows in an adjacent circuit to the reactor. This improves the cooling of the main metallic structures. Since U233 is unavailable, the fuel salt has substituted highly enriched Uranium 238/235. The fuel reprocessing scheme has been demonstrated and improved, leading to efficient recovery of the fuel components, while the behaviour of all fission products in the reprocessing has been evaluated.

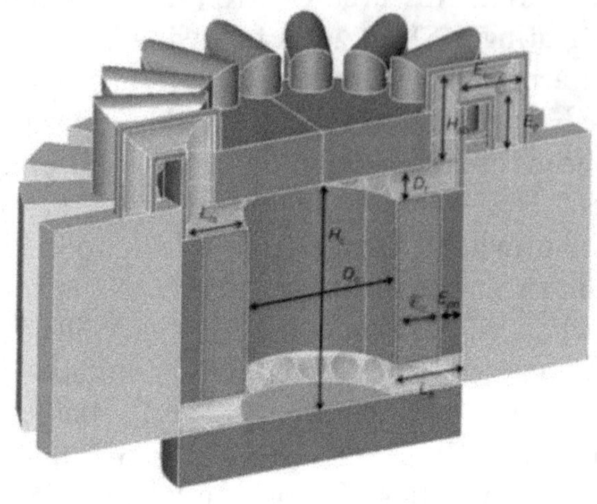

*Figure 13.  MSFR conceptual design (courtesy E. Merle, Laboratoire de Physique Subatomique et de Cosmologie)*

Three types of NiWCr alloys were manufactured in the projects, and an optimised composition for the MSFR has been established. Corrosion studies have demonstrated oxygen and Uranium's role in decreasing corrosion reactions. The key safety features of the MSFR have been analysed and substantiated. Experimental tools for validating simulations have been implemented, and progress has been made in the multiphysics modelling of the core. The current project, SAMOSAFER, is just concluding and has been focused on severe accident modelling and safety assessment for MSR. This four-year project started in 2019 and looked at:

- Freezing of the fuel salt against cold walls and subsequent remelting of the salt;

- Internal heating of the fuel salt causes lower natural circulation and local overheating;

- Overheating of the fuel salt in the MSFR core during transients and in the drain tanks during storage;

- Effects of transients on the thermomechanical integrity of the primary circuit;

- Redistribution of the inventories of radionuclides in the fuel treatment unit via gas bubbling, fluorination and chemical extraction leading to changes in chemistry and mobility of radionuclides.

- The chemistry and physics needed to increase the safety of the MSFR and MSR, in general, were also modelled.

- New safety features to prevent and mitigate severe accidents were also designed, such as an iodine trapping system, an off-gas system and a gas holdup system of the gaseous fission products in the fuel treatment unit, and freeze plugs and drain tanks (for both emergency and normal conditions).

The Euratom programme has done much work on the physical and chemical behaviour of fluoride and chloride salts to close the knowledge gap between the two types and put them on a similarly equal basis to progress to the following stages of building larger experimental reactors. The resulting database is continuously developed, addressing fuel behaviour, fission products, and corrosion interactions.

## Current Challenges to Building Molten Salt Reactors

### Technical

Technical challenges with MSR fall into three broad categories:

I. reactor physics, materials

II. science and salt chemistry

III. and finally, engineering.

In general, the physics of MSR are well understood, and there are no fundamental scientific obstacles to implementing the technology. First is the lack of simulation software that a regulatory body may accept. To build confidence in the software, experimental verification is required. For example, Copenhagen Atomics has built and published simulation models. You can go to their website, download the code, and run it yourself. However, we can only verify that they are correct with experimental steps to collect the data, which would need to be approved by the regulator.

The second factor around salt chemistry and material science is critical and a priority. Gaining

(regulatory) qualification for new structural materials is potentially lengthy and resource-intensive. Accelerating the discovery and testing via multi-scale simulation and machine learning could play a critical role. A better definition of the reactivity between materials and salts is required to drive the selection of materials and candidate salts.

A critical issue concerning the salt phase is the accurate definition of fuel and coolant salts' thermophysical and thermochemical properties. The quality of the existing data is a concern due to the need for more quality assurance protocols and standardised experimental methods to generate these data. Any MSR vendor must create data specific to its salt choice, which is a significant effort. The work done by the JRC could be crucial in this regard.

A validated salt properties database providing data on fuel and coolant salts as a function of salt mixture composition, temperature and pressure can be used as a practical and efficient tool for reactor design and modelling of MSR performance. The prediction of these properties via, for example, molecular dynamics simulations is a second independent tool that can be useful to inform engineering choices during the reactor design phase but will only suffice with validation by regulatory bodies. Thermochemistry data and models that describe the speciation of the fuel, the salt, activation products and fission products will also need development, as they are necessary for performance and safety evaluations.

To mitigate the degradation of structural materials in contact with molten salt, it is paramount to maintain strict control of the salt composition from fuel loading throughout the core lifetime. The compelling challenges here are the definition of manufacturing and purification protocols for the salt compositions, which are needed for a reliable supply chain for the MSR fleet. The salts' purity must be high to prevent radioactive activation and excessive corrosion.

During operation, the salt composition has to be maintained within carefully selected limits. A key aspect of mitigating corrosion is monitoring and controlling the salt redox potential, which has been demonstrated in experiments at a laboratory scale. Still, successful implementation in MSR prototypes presents significant challenges. Electrochemical methods to monitor and alter the oxidative power of the salt anions are still to be demonstrated in prototype setups. Electrochemical setups withstanding highly corrosive and irradiated environments ought to be developed, and their functioning over suitable time frames should be validated.

Reactors using the thorium fuel cycle must include an online fuel salt reprocessing system, which can significantly increase fuel circuit complexity. The functioning of a chemical process unit must be demonstrated to perform sufficiently well in treating highly radioactive material separating nuclear waste from purified fuel. While the processing of a liquid fuel form is greatly simplified compared with the use of solid fuels, the development and potential operational costs of on-site processing systems for proliferation-resistant fuel salt cannot be trivialised.

Lastly, we come to the engineering challenges around MSRs. An environment operating at high temperatures will place thermal stresses on heat exchangers, pumps, mechanical components and vessels. Also, due to self-welding concerns, fluoride salts cannot be used with mechanical valves.

For MSRs, designing a reliable Degassing system to separate gaseous fission products from the fuel represents a key challenge, although some similarities exist with current water-cooled reactors. Degassing represents a convenient feature of liquid fuels. Even though not all MSR concepts rely on it, degassing benefits the neutron economy by removing the neutron poison isotope Xe135, easily separated from the salt because of its very low solubility, and increases the plant safety as no pressure buildup occurs since this isotope does not accumulate within the core. On the other hand, studies from the MSRE (at ORNL) revealed that non-negligible amounts of salt aerosols, solid particulates and mechanically volatilised metal fluoride compounds are directed outside the primary circuit by degassing operations. Together with other naturally volatile radionuclides (e.g. tritium and noble gases), they form a complex feed for any purification system, which poses greater process design challenges.

The design and manufacturing of specific components, for which little prior experience is available, are among the key challenges that MSRs pose. In particular, significant efforts will be required to produce reliable and long-lasting components (such as circulation pumps, heat exchangers, valves and flanges) that are in contact with the harsh salt system. Suitable instrumentation to monitor the status of these components during their lifetimes is yet to be developed and demonstrated. Remote maintenance is required because of the harsh environment, with the consequent rise in the complexity of the operations and cost. Certain MSRs will need components to be replaced periodically, which adds design requirements to allow accessibility to the core for the substitution of degraded or spent components, increasing the overall costs.

## Supply Chain

One problem when building a nuclear power station, you cannot simply order from your local widget supplier. Like the manufacture and repair of aircraft, all the reactor components and materials have strict specifications that must be met, including the nuts and bolts. The supplier must adhere to the necessary assurance and verification processes, such as qualification. MSR is a new technology, so there is no existing supplier base or full technical specifications and assurance checks. In contrast, the current conventional standards are not necessarily directly applicable to MSRs. Oversight of assurance and verification must also be applied by the reactor developer and regulator, which is critical in containing costs by avoiding rectification work due to substandard components/materials.

While for some elements/materials, MSRs could utilise existing commercial-grade suppliers of high-temperature technology used in other industrial processes, this would depend on regulatory approval (more of that later). The problems in the supply chain extend to personnel with knowledge and skills. Some of these (types of ) issues have already been encountered in the UK during the building of Hinckley Point due to the winding down of the existing nuclear industry since the 1990s.

The solution is generating sufficient demand over an extended period to incentivise supply. A requirement for MSR reactors from Europe, the USA, and the UK is enough. However, the challenges that will be faced can easily be seen as we have watched how Western governments have struggled to re-open and ramp up the production of armaments following Russia's invasion of Ukraine. Bureaucratic delays and suppliers' need for concrete contracts before investing represent considerable inertia, and we can anticipate similar problems and delays for MSR procurement.

## Fuel Supply

An MSR using liquid fuel will need a fuel salt specification to support purchasing while fuel salt composition and tolerance standards are still being developed. Other material assurance and verification processes must be designed and implemented, as poor fuel purity adversely significantly affects the corrosion performance of the reactor.

Regulators and government agencies must consider how to authorise the production, transportation and use of fuel salts containing various fissile materials, including enriched Uranium above 5%. A strategic plan for MSR fuel cycles showing where and when materials will be generated, transferred, used, stored and disposed of needs to be developed — just like for any other nuclear fuel. Since the current fuel supply for low-enriched uranium and mixed oxide fuels is based on the solid fuel industry, producing molten salt with uranium, plutonium, or thorium requires new facilities and equipment. Nevertheless, these facilities and equipment are similar to those used in the existing chemical industry. Some MSRs are often compared with chemical reprocessing plants more than with conventional nuclear power plants. As with other supply chain elements, the

same is assumed here: if demand exists, supply will appear.

The investment will be required to develop the infrastructure for reprocessing spent nuclear fuel from stockpiles, making available the fuel salts required for an MSR. On the other hand, reprocessing used nuclear fuel is expected to reduce the amount of radioactive waste for final disposal. This reduction has benefits in several areas, including financial and environmental. Given the overall economic advantages of reprocessing spent nuclear fuel (SNF) via MSR, it is hard to see this investment needing to be more forthcoming once the political will to build MSR and regulatory inertia is overcome. Converting SNF is relatively straightforward, involving dissolving the chopped fuel rods in salts and then removing the contaminants and fission products in much the same process as we have outlined for maintaining the purity of fuel salts in the operating procedures for MSR.

## Maintenance and Operations

In an MSR, it will be necessary to perform fully remote maintenance (of the reactor) because of the high temperature and radioactivity of the fuel. The MSRE, which has operated at ORNL for about four years, is a significant source of documentation and knowledge of the required procedures and tools. Procedures and processes must also be developed for dealing with equipment that is end of life, damaged or needs servicing - and that may be irradiated.  However, improved modelling tools for process operations would facilitate the scale-up and modelling of MSR operations for an extended period (i.e. reactor lifetime) and enable the design and construction of the necessary remote tools that might not currently be available.

## Fuel Salt Waste

Liquid salt does not accumulate physical damage like solid fuel or age. It has an infinite lifespan if its composition can be controlled to remain within a specification. Fission products can potentially build up to equilibrium concentrations, and most designs include continuous, online or batch chemical processing (polishing) of the molten salt. Consequently, MSR fuel salt can be used in future generations of reactors.

Nevertheless, MSRs still require a disposal path for fuel salt waste; defining this path could significantly support the licensing of MSRs. The Office of Nuclear Energy of the United States Department of Energy has recently provided overviews of the potential waste processing and waste form options for MSRs. It has evaluated the status of molten salt waste technologies, focusing on fast spectrum systems.

## Security and Safeguards

Though the current legal framework for IAEA safeguards focuses primarily on existing nuclear power plants and processing facilities, already established methods and practices are expected to apply to MSRs, although adaptation may be necessary. Historically, safeguards and security measures were 'added on' rather than developed concurrently with the first nuclear power plants. Despite this, the safeguards and security measures implemented in conventional nuclear power plants have been effective. This is evident from the lack of severe incidents related to external attacks, sabotage, theft or other diversions of fissile material from commercial nuclear power plants.

Molten salt reactors incorporate features that are fundamentally different from conventional reactors. At the same time, MSRs have limited operational experience and have been restricted to research reactors from a time that precedes modern best practices for safeguards and security. Suppose an MSR is a closed circuit design that actively controls the chemistry of the fuel salt. In that case, it resembles a facility for reprocessing spent nuclear fuel with similar security and safeguarding requirements.

Outside of physical security, the primary challenges are auditing and accounting for all the actinides, fission products, and fissile materials being used, stored, or consumed at all times in the processes. This means analysing the fuel salt dynamically as the reactor operates and accounting for refuelling where fresh fertile or fissile material is added. There are ways to do this, including laser spectroscopy of the fuel salt within the reactor fuel circuit. This is also where detailed chemical and physical models are required so that the actual results can be compared to expected results that allow for the complex chain of reactions that will take place in the reactor.

On the other hand, the transport and handling of nuclear material will increase because of the rapid development and deployment of MSRs and closed nuclear fuel cycles. This will require infrastructure, more personnel capable of dealing with sensitive technology, and a more sophisticated approach to handling bulk nuclear fuels with acceptable verification-activity uncertainties.

Consequently, reactor developers must establish, verify and validate adequate safeguards and security provisions for MSRs. In parallel, regulatory stakeholders — including legislators, international organisations, and national regulators — will need foresight, imagination, and initiative to accommodate proactively the expansion of nuclear power on a large scale, including SMRs and MSRs.

## Regulatory

One of the most significant hurdles potential suppliers/developers must overcome on an SMR is gaining regulatory approval. Each jurisdiction has its own national regulators and legal framework that must be approached. In most instances, it is not just nuclear regulatory hurdles and hoops that must be jumped; for each site, there are likely to be planning and environmental laws and regulations, too. However, we should focus on the nuclear regulators. In that case, we can see that the national structure severely hampers development and innovation because the regulatory mountain has to be climbed in each jurisdiction, multiplies the cost and thus diminishes the returns. Only a large number of projects or sites make sense in this context for it to be viable. Alternatively, you end up with expensive mega projects like Hinckley Point and Sizewell.

While I am not suggesting for a moment that this is an area where we should be cutting corners, it is an area where joint development of agreed standards and mutual recognition would go a long way to mitigating the pain. If an MSR developer could take an approved design from the US to the UK or Europe and vice-versa and go through a streamlined process, it would benefit everyone in reducing costs, which would get passed onto the consumer.

Many of the issues impeding industry interest in MSRs are related to safety evaluation and regulatory licensing tailored to the characteristics of MSRs. Consequently, common safety and licensing challenges exist due to the need for more specific safety evaluation tools and capabilities. The outstanding issues are, among others, the need for a consensus on a set of potential MSR accidents, the form and content of a regulatory licence application, and experimental validation or benchmarks of safety evaluation tools for MSRs. Moreover, current regulatory practices mean accepting newly developed tools is expensive and time-consuming.

The development of licensing standards has started in the USA but has yet to be exhaustive or complete. Some of the required standards for development include the following:

- MSR design safety standards;

- Salt composition standards;

- Fuel salt transportation standards;

- Standard methods for performing the accounting of MSR fissile materials;

- Standard methods for evaluating vital areas of MSRs related to physical protection.

## Next Steps

The near-term deployment of MSRs is potentially viable, as extensive R&D activities have been undertaken. The knowledge gained from the MSRE has been used, and progress has been made with modern research and technology. As a result, various advanced designs have been proposed, and their development continues to be pursued.

Accurate thermohydraulic studies must be carried out to generate data on fluid mechanics and heat transients. Heat and mass transport across the core are set to vary during the fuel cycle as fission products are generated and travel across the fuel circuit. Loop test facilities utilising full-scale components should be developed to test molten salt circulation and purification at time and size scales relevant to commercialisation.

Several accident scenarios must be evaluated independently of the MSR design before commercialisation. To develop accurate source term analysis to gauge performance and safety, developers must describe the chemical speciation and transport behaviour of fission and activation products in the fuel circuit and the containment area. This analysis has to be tailored for non-equilibrium conditions. However, its complexity increases because radionuclide transport across the plant systems within the containment zone changes according to several scenarios. Normal operation with and without an off-gas system, maintenance, abnormal events, and accident scenarios have different complexities.

Inventory procedures for nuclear materials should be addressed in the event of spillage. Furthermore, defining the barriers to preventing the release of radioactive material from liquid fuels is also necessary. Spilling fuel salt during any operation is not especially technically challenging if a catch basin and drain tank (with adequate cooling) are provided. All known designs incorporate this feature. Conceptually, fuel salt flows like water to the drain tank, where it is safely cooled. Some uncertainty remains, however, as to which radionuclides evolve out of the fuel salt during both normal operations and spills.

From a security perspective, approaches to accomplishing the required material control and accountancy at MSRs are still under development, and a consensus has yet to be reached.

To promote public confidence in the technology, developers can focus on producing accurate data about the thermodynamics and chemical speciation of fuel salt mixing with the external atmosphere in the event of loss of coolant accidents. The claims of exceptional solvent ability and inertness of fuel salt should be verified for various spillage scenarios, some general and some specific to an MSR design. Spillage of the fuel salt may also occur as part of monitoring, maintenance or refuelling operations; effective protocols to remediate it have to be demonstrated, although the solidification of the salt matrix is expected to simplify the cleaning of contaminated areas.

# Chapter 6 Economics & Costs of MSR

Finally, it has become time to address the last and most complex criticism of nuclear energy: cost. After safety and waste concerns, the next issue is the public perception of atomic power. Indeed, compared to gas- or coal-powered plants, the cost of legacy and new gigawatt-sized PWR plants would be unfavourable. However, we cannot build more gas-powered plants (leaving aside the energy security questions) due to net zero. However, I am not here to argue about net zero because, in the final analysis, carbon-free becomes a debate about timescales. As stated, intermittent renewables and batteries cannot realistically deliver energy stability. Still, in any case, there is a *positive economic case* to be made for next generation nuclear reactors, including advanced modular reactors (AMR) and small modular reactors (SMR).

To explore the economics of nuclear power, we must look at the composition of the costs of building a nuclear power plant. First (i) is the cost of regulatory approval (of the design). Secondly, (ii) there is the cost of getting permission to use and acquire the site. Third (iii) is the cost of manufacturing, building and bringing to operational readiness. These three major elements must be financed before you make a single penny in revenue. Financing the first three things is the fourth cost and ultimately the largest. It is large because you pay interest on a huge sum for forty years due to the capital borrowed in the first three phases. Repaying the capital outlay is probably not achieved until well into the plant's life. The fifth element (v) is the operational cost and, paradoxically, probably the smallest). Finally (vi), there is the decommissioning cost.

By understanding these elements, we can also consider how government and regulation are placed to mitigate or exacerbate some of these and how we might significantly reduce costs. Lastly, we will also consider the revenue side, which is not just about the electricity that can be generated but also other sources.

Let's start with a *worst case* example: Hinckley Point 'C' (or HPC). This will be the world's second longest nuclear power station build. I believe that the longest build was utterly halted for ten years. Let's contemplate that for a second. Consider the ramifications on cost number 4 - financing. All the time you spend before the plant is operating, you are building debt, interest on the debt and interest on the interest. The quicker you can get to stage 5 - operating, the lower the cost; therefore, to all intents and purposes, time equals cost. Second, consider the circumstances, which is to say that no nuclear power stations have been built in the UK since 1995. That means all the design, construction capability, and supply chains have simply dissipated. Likewise, with the human capital, all the scientists and engineers have retired or moved on. All of these things take time and cost money to rebuild. Lastly, the scale of the project, containing two huge reactors, imposes its own costs, although when the cost is spread over the power generated, it is less per MWh. The public perception is always the headline cost, which is a vast number indeed. In January 2024 (literally, as I was writing this), EDF announced that costs would rise to £35bn (adjusted for inflation) and operation would be delayed to at least 2029.

HPC is built to the European Pressurised Reactor (EPR) design, and it includes new features to meet the stringent safety requirements of the German government in particular. For example, there is a double concrete building shell to protect against potential aircraft impact, and no fewer than four different types of independent cooling systems are provided. These cooling systems are there to prevent accidental damage to the reactor core (and therefore the risk of radioactive material escaping into the environment) in case of a natural disaster, equipment failure or human error.

As previously mentioned, the price we will pay for energy is £92.50 per MWh at 2012 prices (if the actual price paid falls below this, then the Treasury /taxpayer funds the shortfall, and vice-versa, the extra accrues to the Treasury). This is known as a Contract for Difference or CfD, and the contract amount (£92.50 /MWh) is called the strike price, which increases with inflation (CPI) each year. For comparison, snapshot data from the National Grid Live shows that over the past year (2023), the average price paid for electricity was £91.62.MWh, where for HPC, after adjusting for inflation, it would be £123. Given the reliability of nuclear power, that begins to seem reasonable, as the costs for wind (see Chapter 2), over which we have no control over the amount of energy generated, are not dissimilar.

If the time taken to get HPC operational is disastrous for costs, so is the method of financing. As we mentioned, the National Audit Office (NAO) has criticised the government for financing this privately. Thus, the project's risks fall on the supplier (EdF). From one point of view, that was wise, given all the overruns. Still, the only way for EDF to finance the massive debt was to borrow expensively at commercial rates and pass the cost onto the consumer via a price negotiated through the CfD. EdF knew this was a big, risky project that would be expensive to finance, so it negotiated a higher price accordingly. In other words, the price we will be paying for the electricity generated reflects the magnitude of the risks. The government can borrow at much cheaper rates than a commercial entity like EdF; in 2016 these were still at rock bottom. However, as we know, that particular worm has now turned. This forced the NAO to conclude we could build several HPCs for the same amount if the government had financed the project directly [29]. However, the government doesn't want to do this because it would be counted in the state debts, reducing the amount they could spend on other things such as welfare.

| Attribution of Strike Price | £ / MWh | % of CfD Price |
|---|---|---|
| Construction Risk Premium | 35 | 38 |
| Other financing | 26 | 29 |
| Ops and Maintenance | 19.5 | 21 |
| Capital Cost | 11 | 12 |
| TOTAL | 92.5 | 100 |

***Fig 14.  Attribution of CfD Strike Price  by EdF***

You can see from the table above the actual proportion of the strike price paid by consumers that were eaten up by all the types of financing was around 2/3 of the total. Therefore, the state has developed a new funding method known as a regulated asset base (RAB [28]). This will be potentially used to finance Sizewell C when a decision is finally taken in 2024. RAB methods allow for sharing risks between the supplier and the consumer by allowing the developer to draw on a flow of funds during the build that is offset against future electricity supplies.   Funds can be drawn for "appropriately incurred development costs", and these assets are added to the regulated register. This only happens at/after a project is approved to proceed. This could, or should, make the financing cheaper and reduce some of the risks for developers. We will compare each method of financing later in the chapter.

The third factor that makes HPC particularly troublesome is the sheer scale of the project and the actual design. The design based on the European Pressurised Water Reactor has encountered several problems where it has been deployed at other plants, creating delays and cost overruns at these. Mega projects such as HPC create their own set of unique challenges. Examples include lifting the massive roof for the reactor and putting it in place, constructing a sea wall to protect the plant from any Fukushima style tsunami (not a noted UK phenomenon), and a billion-gallon pond to flood the reactor to prevent any meltdowns. Dealing with builds on this scale means you must create unique pieces of engineering equipment to complete the project - you get the opposite of economies of scale and factory production line processes. Whenever we think about major infrastructure projects from the Queen Elizabeth line (Crossrail) to HS2, there are always massive delays and resulting cost overruns. This isn't surprising because it can take a year to refurbish a footbridge over a railway, and the overall reduction in UK productivity in engineering projects due to additional regulatory and safety requirements.

In summary, there have been a number of issues explicitly contributing to the high cost at HPC:

- Mega construction project - with resulting incremental complexity

- Troubled new design that needed over 7,000 changes

- Costly financing

Sizewell should go more smoothly due to a stable design and learning experiences from HPC. However, it would still suffer from some of the drawbacks inherent in the EPR design, including size and scale.

# Reducing the cost of nuclear building programmes

What can we do instead to reduce the cost and risk of a nuclear building programme? First, we can start with the cost of producing and approving designs. The design always varies slightly with all the mega-scale power plants as kinks are ironed out. Improvements are made, and this invariably continues to some extent right through from initial approval of the design through the build phase as subsequent design iterations are created, therefore keeping the reactor size down and reusing the design in a highly repeatable way would reduce the risks and costs.

## Rationalise the Approval Process

Firstly, we should rationalise the approval process. If a design is approved by a US or EC regulatory body, it should be treated as approved for use in the UK and vice-versa. This could be achieved by sharing and agreeing on the approval criteria. This would be a huge cost saving for 4th generation reactor designs, especially molten salts, which are at the early stages of this process. This would also encourage the cross-national use of designs with corresponding efficiency savings due to the reuse of designs. The use of small and modular reactors would leverage this benefit the most.  The cost of the design and approval is effectively spread over the number of reactors deployed. If SMRs are deployed in large numbers, the cost per unit, hence the cost per GWh of electricity generated, drops dramatically. This (and the acquired human capital) is why EDF have suggested that power prices and costs would fall significantly for Sizewell C (using essentially the same designs as HPC). Imagine leveraging this over dozens or even hundreds of reactors.

The second cost element involves the approval of the site. The UK has numerous sites of old/existing nuclear plants with all the required infrastructure—connections to the grid and road and rail links to facilitate construction. Usually, existing sites will meet considerably lower levels of objections from residents. These old sites can be redesignated for new plants. There are about sixteen potential sites which fall into this category, some more and some less suitable.  4th generation and SMR designs are much more efficient regarding land use, meaning a higher power density per acre can be achieved.

In the UK, we can designate infrastructure projects as having ("strategic importance". If projects are thus defined in the national plan, they enjoy a slightly more streamlined planning process, meaning local objections can be more easily overruled. We should designate all nuclear builds as strategic.

We should also examine how we could further reduce the planning process so we don't require 350,000 page planning submissions, as is the case for Sizewell. Where existing nuclear sites are being reused, I don't see any reason not to reduce this to almost a formality.

*"The UK government is now holding a consultation to establish a new approach to siting nuclear power stations. The current approach was set by the energy national policy statement in June 2011, which confirmed that eight sites are suitable for new nuclear power stations by 2025 – all are the sites of existing nuclear plants."* [31]

In addition to these large multi-gigawatt sites, we should consider the feasibility of siting SMR close to industrial sites with high energy consumption levels, thus reducing transmission infrastructure and losses. These locations could include steel and chemical plants and refineries, as well as places with high densities of data centres.

## Reduce the Build Cost

The third cost element to tackle is build.  The new 4th generation reactors, with their passive safety systems, would eliminate the need to build vast stores of water to flood the reactor and massive sea walls to stop (non-existent?) tsunamis. Adopting these reactor designs would significantly reduce the engineering elements required for active safety systems.

Lastly, the potential use of small modular reactors facilitates scaled-up production processes that bring economies of scale to the production of the reactor parts.  This could apply to the entire power production cycle, as found in smaller combined cycle gas-fired systems.  For example, Copenhagen Atomics has produced a reactor design housed in a standard-sized shipping container.  The reactor is built off-site, fueled and shipped to the deployment location, where it is 'plugged' into the power generation system. All fueling and maintenance are carried out off-site at centralised facilities.  Remember that a major proportion of the cost of a nuclear powered plant producing electricity is the electricity generating part.  Once you move past the heat exchanger element, components similar to those in a conventional thermal power station can be used.

Although nuclear sceptics have tried to downplay the cost savings that could be achieved with SMR, which is still unproven, mass production techniques, have reduced costs in every industry where they have been applied.  This includes building modular houses, where cost and timelines were reduced and quality improved. Many companies, including Rolls-Royce, have stood behind the principle and are prepared to back themselves financially if they get regulatory approval.

One of the problems with building multi-gigawatt reactors has been the cost overruns associated with the build. It would be the case with SMR that the reactors would be supplied at fixed costs with the (smaller) risks assumed by the supplier. Although EDF has assumed some of the cost overrun from HPC, they had to achieve a very high fixed price for the electricity generated to assume this risk. If the risk of cost overruns on the reactor build were minimised by using SMR built at an industrial scale, then this risk premium, which the consumer ultimately bears, would be eliminated.

## Reduce Finance Cost

This brings us to the financing cost of nuclear power. As we have already discussed, the major cost element is raising the capital and covering the interest charges over 20 to 30 years. The amount of capital required depends on the design, planning, buying/preparing of the site, and the build cost up to the operational phase. We have just discussed how these elements could be significantly reduced. However, a major variable is the amount of interest that must be paid in capital. The rate of interest that lenders /investors will require will be determined by their perception of the risk of default, that is, not being able to repay the principal (the amount borrowed), not being able to cover the interest payments, or even worse the need to raise further capital (due to delays in making the asset operational or other cost overruns).

There is no shortage of capital globally for borrowers regarded as very low risk. There is a significant appetite for debt (or equity) that can make stable, guaranteed payments, which aligns well with the liability side of things like pension funds. With this in mind, then it is governments (especially developed Western ones) that pay the lowest rates of interest on their debts because they are regarded as having a low risk of default. Investors are happy to lend money to governments for 20 to 30 years, secure that they will receive all the interest payments and get the return of the capital at the end of the period. Very highly rated and secure companies with a good track record will pay a small premium over government debt, with the premium rising the worse the company's credit rating.

*"EDF Energy is currently constructing Hinkley Point C nuclear power station in Somerset. In this case, EDF is liable for all construction costs, including delays. The company will only be able to recoup the rewards from the investment when, or if, the plant starts generating electricity.*

*The government has assured EDF of long-term funding via the contract for difference (CfD) – a legal agreement through which the difference between the opening and closing trade prices is paid." [35]*

As we have seen from the example of HPC, building a first-of-its-kind (in the UK) nuclear power station is likely to run into considerable delays and overruns. They are often doubling the cost (or worse). This does not make for a very good case for investors when a commercial company seeks to borrow money, which leads to them demanding high interest rates to cover the risk.  Ultimately, the electricity consumers, i.e., you and me, must pay all these costs. These costs are passed on as charges for the electricity we consume via higher CfDs.

It may be stating the obvious, but many electricity consumers are taxpayers too, and we pay our taxes to the government. Therefore, it is legitimate to ask why the government cannot borrow the money when the UK Treasury will be charged the lowest rates of interest to borrow. In this case, the government would act on behalf of the ultimate beneficiaries, the taxpayers/consumers. This happens with infrastructure such as roads and rail, so why not other critical infrastructure? We will return to the different financing options later in the chapter. Still, reducing and managing the cost of financing is crucial to reducing the cost for consumers. This can seen in the chart below. This (Fig 15) argues that financing costs carried by the state for infrastructure is a social cost that should be excluded for cost comparison. Put another way, it is an investment on which society will eventually make a return, like the cost of educating the young.

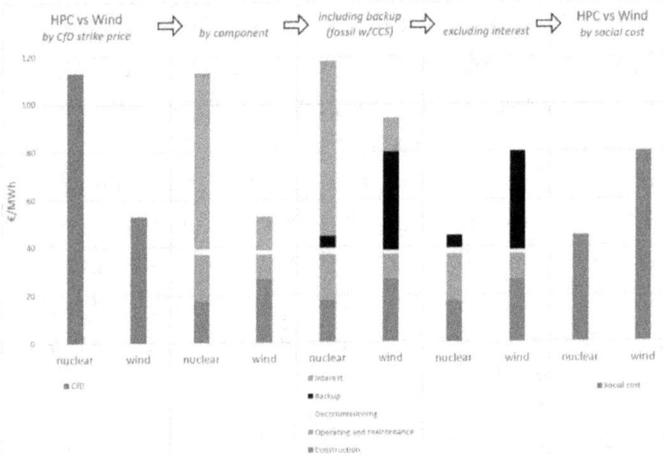



Figure 15. Relative cost of HPC Vs Wind source The Kernel 2019, Joris Van Dorp [41]

## HPC Lifetime Relationship to Cost

When people say that nuclear power is expensive, they generally react to a headline figure for the cost of the plant. However, there are better measures of whether it is costly. To be expensive or cheap is relative to something else. The only way to compare is apples with apples, or how much electricity is generated £ for £.

So, how much electricity will HPC generate? Well, this depends on how long it will run for. The lifetime design of the plant is 60 years. However, it could run for 80 years as many previous nuclear plants, Magnox, and advanced gas-cooled reactors (AGR) have exceeded their design lifetime by 20 years (half as long again). This would make a big difference to the cost equation.

So HPC generating 3.2 GWh or electricity with 95% efficiency will generate (3,200MWh x 24 x 365 x 60 x 95%)  approximately 1,597,824 GWh over its design lifetime. Given the last projected cost of £35bn, this gives a cost of £21.90 per MWh, which we have seen is positively cheap compared to the cost of offshore wind (last CfD £73 MWh). It is worth noting that the life of a wind turbine will be much shorter, only 20-25 years, with high maintenance costs for the blades during its life.

## HPC Decommissioning Costs

The more astute among you will realise that decommissioning costs will also be significant and that these should be factored into the costs. It should also be noted that EdF has fully costed for this and set aside the relevant funds to pay for it under the terms of its licence. [36].

The cost of the decommissioning (estimated to be £7.2bn) has been factored in at £2 per MWh and is part of the strike price in the CfD [37]. If costs are forecast to increase, then EdF will have to set aside more funds from the revenue.

## HPC Operating cost

After commissioning the plant, the operating costs are estimated at between £11 and £20  per MWh.

This includes all running costs during operation, including personnel costs, fuel costs, permits, insurance, maintenance, taxes and the processing and, importantly, the ultimate disposal of nuclear waste. This will be comparable to offshore wind and cheaper than fossil fuels. Because HPC uses solid fuel rods and is not a breeder reactor, operating costs will be higher than those of molten salt reactors with a potentially cheaper fuel cycle. According to OECD's publications, fuel costs are estimated to be around £9 MWh for this technology.[40]

**This gives us a total cost of c. £40 per MWh (£21.90 + £2 + £15.5), which is lower than with other forms of electricity generation [38], including wind or fossil fuel.**

What happens to the £52.5 / MWh difference between this cost and the strike price (£92.50)? Well, this will be paid as a premium (interest, dividend or other forms of profit distribution) to the investors and lenders of HPC, namely the (pension) funds and (state) participations of France and China, who are the owners of the project. The UK government had prohibited itself from participating in nuclear energy investment for antinuclear political reasons. However, that policy appears to have softened in recent years, as noted in the NAO report on HPC, which we mentioned.

## HPC Total Gross Profit

Another way to look at HPC would be to consider how much gross profit it will likely make. We have already established that all the costs come to £40 MWh. If we assume that the revenue generated from the electricity achieves the same average that was paid to generators throughout 2023, which is £73 MWh (less than the CfD), then over the 1,600 TWh the gross profit over its lifetime is approximately £53bn (in today's money). That is slightly less than £1bn per year, which is not bad for a long-term inflation-proofed return on an original £35bn investment.

## Levelised Costs of Electricity (LCOE)

To get an objective comparison of different forms of power generation, we will have to turn to publicly available reports that compare them using a like-for-like method called the Levelised Cost of Electricity (LCOE).  LCOE provides a straightforward way of consistently comparing the costs of different generating technologies, focusing on the costs incurred by the generator over the plant's lifetime. LCOE is presented as the average discounted cost per MWh generated. The simplicity of the system means that there are factors which are not considered, including a technology's broader impact given the timing, location, and other characteristics of its generation. For example, a wind plant built a long distance from centres of high demand will increase the load on the transmission network. LCOE considers the costs of planning, construction, operation, and carbon emissions, reflecting the cost of building, operating and decommissioning a generic plant for each technology. Potential revenue streams are not considered, except for heat revenues for Combined Heat Plants.

The following table shows the LCOE for different generating types coming from the US but shows advanced nuclear costs, offshore wind, and solar.

| Plant type | Capacity factor (percent) | Levelized capital cost | Levelized fixed O&M[a] | Levelized variable cost | Levelized transmission cost | Total system LCOE or LCOS |
|---|---|---|---|---|---|---|
| **Dispatchable technologies** | | | | | | |
| Ultra-supercritical coal | 85% | $52.11 | $5.71 | $23.67 | $1.12 | $82.61 |
| Combined cycle | 87% | $9.36 | $1.68 | $27.77 | $1.14 | $39.94 |
| Advanced nuclear | 90% | $60.71 | $16.15 | $10.30 | $1.08 | $88.24 |
| Geothermal | 90% | $22.04 | $15.18 | $1.21 | $1.40 | $39.82 |
| Biomass | 83% | $40.80 | $18.10 | $30.07 | $1.19 | $90.17 |
| **Resource-constrained technologies** | | | | | | |
| Wind, onshore | 41% | $29.90 | $7.70 | $0.00 | $2.63 | $40.23 |
| Wind, offshore | 44% | $103.77 | $30.17 | $0.00 | $2.57 | $136.51 |
| Solar, standalone[c] | 29% | $26.60 | $6.38 | $0.00 | $3.52 | $36.49 |
| Solar, hybrid[c,d] | 28% | $34.98 | $13.92 | $0.00 | $3.63 | $52.53 |
| Hydroelectric[d] | 54% | $46.58 | $11.48 | $4.13 | $2.08 | $64.27 |
| **Capacity resource technologies** | | | | | | |
| Combustion turbine | 10% | $53.78 | $8.37 | $45.83 | $9.89 | $117.86 |
| Battery storage | 10% | $64.03 | $29.64 | $24.83 | $10.05 | $128.55 |

Source: U.S. Energy Information Administration, *Annual Energy Outlook 2022*

*Figure 16. Estimated unweighted levelised cost of electricity (LCOE) and levelised cost of storage (LCOS) for new resources entering service in 2027 (2021 dollars per megawatt hour) [39].*

This probably understates the cost of gas-fuelled power as this cost tends to be lower in the US due to the amount of shale gas available. Also note that hybrid solar costs only provide balancing power for a few hours, not days. Lastly, this data was prepared in 2022, and costs for offshore wind have risen dramatically since then, but solar costs have continued to fall.

The UK government published a study in 2023 [38] that suggested the LCOE of offshore wind was about £43 MWh and the cost of a CCGT £114 Mwh. However, this research appears to be what caused them to set the maximum bid price in the 2023 capacity auctions at that level. In turn, that gave rise to exactly zero bids, which pretty conclusively demonstrates it was either wrong in the first place or simply out of date, with rising costs specific to (offshore) wind power generation making bids at £44MWh uneconomic.

In the above table (Figure 16), "combustion turbine" refers to gas-fired plants that are specifically used to balance the grid during periods of peak demand. They can come on the grid faster than other thermal plants, like combined cycle or coal. Battery storage and combustion turbines are used to balance the grid and are essential to balance intermittent resources like solar and wind if the grid is not to collapse. Therefore, when considering these technologies, the cost must also include the cost of balancing technologies.

For example, if we require a steady 1 MWh of power (and never less from) offshore wind, we would also require balancing power from batteries or gas. However, this means we incur the whole capital cost of having that standby power even if it is only used around half the time. Thus, if we choose the cheapest option (combustion turbine), the actual cost of offshore wind is $190.29 ($136.51 + $53.78 ) to have this alternative just standing by until the wind fails.

This gives us the following relative costs:

| | |
|---|---|
| Onshore wind + combustion | $94.01 |
| Offshore wind + combustion | $190.29 |
| Offshore wind + Battery | $200.54 |
| Solar standalone + Battery | $165.04 |
| 4th gen Nuclear power | $88.24 |

From this, we can begin to see the lie that renewables are the cheapest and best way to become free from fossil fuels. In fact it makes a mockery of our entire energy strategy for the past twenty years.

Another 2015 study compares renewables plus storage, nuclear, and fossil fuels with and without carbon capture and storage. The study finds that, for the scenarios considered, costs were similar at about 84 /MWh at up to 50% renewables and rose for renewables above an 80% share as grid-scale storage, imports, and tidal range generation were applied.[44]

## Different Financing Models for Nuclear

As we discussed earlier in the chapter, the financing of the project is the largest element of cost [41]. Therefore, we should consider the pros and cons of the different potential approaches as this will determine the cost of electricity production. There are three potential models to consider:

- Direct funding by the treasury

- Design-Build-Finance-Maintain-Operate (DBFMO) a.k.a. Private Public Partnership (PPP), a.k.a. Public Finance Initiative, a.k.a. CfD

- Regulated Asset Base Model (RAB)

- A hybrid model that we shall call PPP-RAB

## Direct Funding

The traditional approach to investing in infrastructure relies on the government using revenue (from taxes or borrowing) to finance new or upgraded infrastructure. Although the design and construction can be procured through competitive tenders from private firms, the traditional model relies on continued government ownership and operation once construction is completed. In recent decades, many governments have responded to the limitations of this model through private sector involvement in the funding, financing, delivery and operation of infrastructure.

The two primary challenges with the traditional model driving this change are:

- Difficulty in finding sufficient government finance, either because of weakness in tax

> revenue or a reluctance (or inability) to increase government borrowing

- Evidence (or policy preference) shows that government ownership and operation of infrastructure assets results in worse price and/or quality outcomes than the private sector.

HS2 was funded through direct government grants, which appear on the balance sheets and needed funding from current government expenditure. This is one reason why when the project cost kept rising, the government could no longer afford it and scrapped further phases. Furthermore, any cost overruns come back to the politicians' doors, and they don't like this. It makes them look inadequate or incompetent. This is why they seek to push these risks onto someone else, but as a result, the project costs more to finance to compensate for the construction risk. However, it does illustrate that a project can be funded directly if there is a will to do so.

Fundamentally, the problem with this method arises because the government (whatever hue) does not have the money to fund the necessary infrastructure projects. It is borrowing money hand over fist to fund the welfare state, with a budget deficit running around a significant 3pc of GDP and with taxes at an already 70-year high. The first casualty of any spending cuts is *always* infrastructure projects, as they are easiest to cut, and there are fewer howls of outrage than removing benefits (entitlements?). The (now last)

Conservative government's pledge to build 40 new hospitals is a perfect example. With the demise of the Private Finance Initiatives (PFI) in 2018 [32], there has been a struggle to achieve the funding needed to deliver this (key) pledge.

The question of why the government does not borrow more money to invest in public infrastructure, such as nuclear, will no doubt arise. After all, the UK stock of capital infrastructure and investment has steadily declined over the past three decades and is the lowest G7 country for 24 out of 30 years [34]. Gordon Brown did the country no favours in the long term by deliberately confusing spending with investment (using the terms interchangeably), which goes to the root of the problem.   The government taxes or borrows money and then decides how to spend it. It puts the money into separate accounts, one for investment and another for spending.  However, if it (sensibly) pledged to "spend" from current income and only borrow to "invest", it wouldn't solve the problem as the benefits from investments do not necessarily deliver hard cash in return.  For example, education - spending or investment? A hospital is an asset, but the NHS does not directly derive revenue from it. Likewise, a road generates a financial benefit. Still, the revenue cannot be separated from other income unless you can charge a toll for it. Therefore, much "investment" is ultimately subject to the same constraints as spending. Those constraints are the perception of the government's ability to meet the interest bill.

Investors buying government bonds like to see that future finances are on a healthy trajectory that will see them safely repaid. This is debatable for most G7 governments (including the US and Japan). As we saw from the fiasco of the so-called Truss mini-budget, any loss of confidence can lead to a rapidly spiralling financial crisis.

## CfD / PFI / PPP Financing

PFIs were a mechanism by which private companies undertook funding for the building and operations of public assets for a guaranteed revenue stream, which the Treasury/taxpayer ultimately guaranteed. These fell into disrepute [32] [33], with the collapse of the contractor Carillion in 2018 leaving two unfinished hospitals as the final straw. Whether these schemes were good value for the taxpayer or not (and arguably, there is insufficient data to determine this [32]), then at least they achieved the objective of delivering hundreds of projects, mainly on time and within budget. Without PFI, most of these projects would never have been delivered at all; however, the abiding public impression is that the lifetime cost was inordinately high.

 One of the significant criticisms of PFI was that the cost of financing was treated as level over the life of the asset. This meant that once the risky stages of the project had been completed and it was operating if it did not overrun or overspend, the asset could be refinanced at a cheaper rate. This profit would accrue to the operator (PFI company). This leads to potential excess profits and excessive costs for the consumer (ultimately, you and me).  The cheapest form of financing will always be direct government borrowing. If this is not available and will be shifted off the government balance sheet, then the cost will depend on where the risk sits. It will be very expensive if it sits almost entirely with the private enterprise. If some of these risks are mitigated via a government guarantee or something similar, they will be proportionally reduced. This is where the RAB model comes from.

The CfD model is equivalent to PPP/PFI but for revenue-generating projects. The approach is identical: the private partner(s) design-build-finance-manage-operate the asset. Still, instead of receiving fixed revenue payments, they receive a guaranteed minimum price for electricity via the CfD. Arguably, in the case of HPC, the risk premium has been fully utilised/justified, as EdF has had to suck up the cost overruns.

The efficiency gains in the CfD/PPP approach are primarily determined at a single point in time: by competition between the bidders for the contract (ex-ante).  This only works well when there is de-facto a single bidder. For example, EdF for HPC. However, it clearly works better when there is competition from multiple suppliers for multiple licences, such as in the bidding for wind licences.

## Regulated Asset Base (RAB) - A Financing alternative to PFI for Revenue generating assets

In the RAB model, private (or corporatised state-owned) companies act as the infrastructure manager: they own, invest in and operate infrastructure assets. The infrastructure manager receives charges revenue from users and subsidies to fund its operations and recoup investment costs. The infrastructure manager would behave like a natural monopoly without regulation – setting prices too high to earn "exceptional" profits. An economic regulator is therefore established to provide efficiency incentives and to cap prices, revenue, and rate of return received by the infrastructure manager to improve social welfare. Efficiency incentives aim to mimic the incentives the market would face if it were competitive. In this case, the efficiency gains arise primarily through the interaction between the regulator and the infrastructure manager "during the contract".

The RAB is already widely used in the UK for water, gas, and electricity networks.

Applied to nuclear projects, consumers' payments would be used to release revenue during plant construction. According to proponents of the RAB, ongoing revenue from taxpayers would:

- Reduce the cost of capital

- Attract more investors

- Deliver affordable and reliable nuclear power.

Compared to the RAB, the contracts for difference (CfD) model requires that developers finance the construction of a nuclear project and bear the associated risks. Under a CfD, the developer agrees to pay the entire plant construction cost in return for the "strike price" for electricity output when the plant starts generating power.

The Nuclear Energy (Financing) Act 2022 came into force on 31 March 2022 after the abandonment of three large new nuclear developments at Moorside in 2018 and Wylfa Newydd and Oldbury B in 2020 because the developers were unable to attract finance for the developments.

The power and utilities executive at Barclays Bank described the RAB model as providing "a high level of certainty and confidence and predictability for investors" and "structured to produce attractive, stable, low-risk and inflation-linked returns at scale". A Government Support Package would be provided to give investors protection from specified low probability but high impact risks that the private sector would not be able to support, including the risk of cost overrun above a remote threshold, disruption to debt markets, some risks for which insurance is not available, and *political* risks.

The main feature of RAB is that it involves consumers paying from the start of construction for benefits they will only begin to receive when construction is completed and the plant produces electricity. One of the critical questions that should be answered in assessing whether a RAB-funded project should go ahead is whether the eventual benefit consumers could receive, in this case through cheaper electricity charges in the long run, is enough to compensate them for the opportunity cost of the payments made while receiving no benefit. This is a long winded way of saying that project finance costs are directly relational to the time it takes to deliver.

When considering the business case (whether the benefits outweigh the costs), it will depend on the assumption of the discount rate (or the rate of return demanded by the consumer/investor) and the planned duration.

The central advantage of RAB is that it offers one of the lowest financing costs in developed economies, only marginally above that of government bonds. At the same time, incentive regulation can provide adjustable high-powered incentives for operational efficiency during the life of the infrastructure. One of the more significant challenges of RAB is incentivising efficient capital expenditures, which is a problem that appears to be more adequately solved in PPPs. These are well established for delivering projects on time and on budget; however, the cost of financing PPPs is substantially higher than for RAB, and the PPP contract is considered relatively rigid during operations.

At its worst, the RAB has been called an "open chequebook" that incentivises developers to overspend on construction. Particularly for large and complex nuclear projects, these costs may be too difficult to regulate fairly since investors may benefit when projects go wrong. Over time, this system may create more financial complexity while reducing project delivery and regulatory efficiency incentives. Through it all, taxpayers are left to cover the accumulating costs.

The RAB model hasn't yet been used in the UK nuclear industry. For a smaller-scale application of the RAB in the UK, many experts point toward the Thames Tideway Tunnel project (TTT), a £4.2 billion sewer project with a planned completion date by 2025.

The TTT is a worthwhile investment on paper, but the project is not without its critics. Under the RAB model, the amount customers will pay for tunnel construction remains to be determined. The estimated cost of the TTT is £4.2 billion, much smaller than large-scale nuclear projects like Sizewell.

## Hybrid RAB - CfD

We should ask whether it is feasible and desirable to merge the advantages of both approaches – the low cost of finance and continuous incentives for operational efficiency in the RAB, with efficiency in infrastructure delivery of the CfD/PFI – into a single model.

The RAB (Regulated Asset Base) and PFI/CfD (a.k.a. PPP) models use a contractual framework designed to address the time-risk inconsistency problem associated with infrastructure investment. Building infrastructure is high risk, while operating it is low risk. However, the RAB approach has a potential drawback in that it can be challenging to establish appropriate benchmarks and incentives to avoid the open chequebook issue and necessitates an economic regulator. On the other hand, the PFI/CfD model encounters challenges such as fewer incentives to achieve the lowest strike price for the electricity and reduced flexibility during the operational phase. Moreover, CfD typically involves a *significantly higher* financing cost than the RAB model.

A primary concern regarding the RAB approach is that it may lead to excessive capital expenditures, thereby gradually increasing the base upon which returns are calculated. In contrast, the PFI/CfD model's complexity, long-term contractual commitments, and inherent uncertainties raise doubts about whether competition will lead to efficient and cost-effective investments. In other words, the main issue with PFI/CfDs is related to the required returns and, potentially, the investment base. An example is the failed Offshore wind auction in 2023/4 that led to no bids at the maximum price, which the regulator had calculated was fair. This gave rise to almost doubling the allowed maximum the following year to try and attract bidders.

Current evidence suggests that the concerns associated with PFI/CfD returns and the capital expenditure (capex) risk premiums demanded by construction-operating companies are significantly greater than the perceived capex bias in the RAB model. This capex premium in CfD arises due to risk aversion and construction risk transfer through fixed-price and fixed-date contracts. If a regulated company adopted a similar contracting approach, a comparable capex premium would likely be observed due to the transferred construction risk.

In the RAB model, the capex bias results from regulated companies aiming to construct assets to a higher quality standard than necessary, as indicated by life-cycle cost optimisation or cost overruns. The economic regulator's role is to mitigate such excesses. Additionally, in the RAB model, the regulator provides operational efficiency incentives to the infrastructure manager. In contrast, PPPs generally lack such incentives throughout the long lifespan of the assets, with any contractual adjustments usually incurring additional costs for the government.

In summary, while both models offer efficiency advantages over traditional approaches, particularly in reducing excessive employment, the critical question is the allocation of risk. It is most efficient to allocate the risk to the party with the greatest tolerance, which their efficiency or cost of delivery can determine.

One solution would be to use a Special Purpose Vehicle (SPV), which would be state-owned and backed, to raise the Capital (using bonds - fixed interest) finance. The SPV would then contract out for all the different stages of the project and ultimately derive the revenue to repay the bond investors' fixed amounts. Excess profit (dividends) over the cost of repaying bondholders, or ultimately losses, would end up with the Treasury, who would be the ultimate owner/equity holder. This is a principle similar to Contracts for Difference (CfD), which are given to wind and solar farm operators under the current bidding schemes where the revenue excess or shortfall ends with the Treasury. The difference is the operator bears much of the execution and operational risk of the project/asset in a CfD scheme.

In contrast, the state bears more risk of using an SPV, but the finance cost would be much lower, leading to cheaper electricity. The risk to the Treasury/taxpayer is managed by chunking the project delivery into stages and contracting out different parts at fixed prices. Let us look at how this could work.

Great Britsh Nuclear (GBN) could be used to manage all the functions of the SPV (although the SPV would be a separate legal entity for each plant). The risks around the project would be reduced, splitting the project into the phases described previously in Chapter 6. The site would be bought and ultimately operated by GBN, with a third-party contractor preparing it for a fixed price. GBN would also manage the planning approval process. The government has a significant role in pushing through this part of the process with the minimum delay as part of the strategic infrastructure initiatives. GBN would then contract a commercial company with a pre-approved generic reactor design to build and install the reactor for a fixed price. They would also contract with a commercial power company (as you would for a conventional thermal power plant) for the turbines and electrical generators compatible with the reactor (the secondary heat exchangers). Operating the plant would also be contracted out for a fixed price if desired (usually to the company that built it). The operations could also be further split between the nuclear reactor element and the power generation.

To provide clarity to the bond investors and the Treasury that they would get their money back (the former) or not be forced to pick up losses (the latter), the regulator/government could give a fixed price contract (rising with CPI) for the electricity that will be generated for 30 years to the SPV. This could be based on the average strike price for electricity in the year prior to the project being approved. We calculated the likely value of this for a reactor like HPC in Chapter 6. This clarity helps to make the risks transparent and thus brings down the costs (of financing). Overall, it makes sense to structure the borrowing so that the bonds can be redeemed in tranches through the plant's operating life, leaving a sufficient period to accumulate funds towards decommissioning.

An alternative approach, for example, with the cost of preparing the site for the installation, could be met from private finance, where an agreed rent would be paid by the SPV (with the Treasury picking up the risk of default). The SPV would competitively tender and contract with operators to build, install, and operate reactor(s) and generation equipment, which could do this at a fixed price for installation and ongoing fees for operating to service level agreements (SLA). The SPV would raise the finance for installation, pay the operators and collect the revenue from the electricity. Ultimately, all the assets are owned by the SPV / Treasury. With long-term arrangements for operating the asset based on SLA for delivering power (thermal and electric, respectively), private operators would have sufficient incentives to avoid skimping in either build or maintenance.

We have demonstrated that nuclear power mega projects can be competitive on costs over their life (c.f. Chapter 6), and if it was financed differently, it could even be a good deal for consumers. Now, we should consider even more positive possibilities. At this point, I will use specific examples as this company is transparent, and the relevant information is available in the public domain.

The CEO of Copenhagen Atomics recently stated that his product was *beyond* 4th generation and small modular, that he could achieve stable, reliable power generation at GW scale for a cost of £15 - £30 MWh (electric, not just heat). Copenhagen Atomics (CA) would build, install, and operate the plant at this price. They would also undertake the decommissioning of the reactors. No public investment would be required outside of regulatory approval and siting and they match any electric generating investment on price. Because this power is stable but potentially load-following, it is very valuable for the grid, much more so than a corresponding amount of wind or solar energy. CA would not operate the conventional part of the electricity generating cycle, only the nuclear part.

We have already reviewed the CA reactor proposal in the chapter on reactor types and designs. The CA reactor is a Thorium breeder reactor moderated with heavy water and has a very high neutron efficiency. The reactor and primary heat exchanger are contained within a box the size of a shipping container so it can be easily handled and transported. All radioactive elements are circulated within this secure container. The reactor can initially be fuelled from radioactive active waste, so it is also a burner reactor that extracts 10x more energy from the waste fuel than originally produced. CA is keen to use UK plutonium stocks to initially fuel the reactor to start the Thorium-Uranium breeding cycle.

Uranium solid fuel reactors vs CA thorium reactor
CAPEX not included

| Old vs new | Solid fuel reactors | CA thorium reactor | Difference |
| --- | --- | --- | --- |
| Expected plant life | 60 years + extension | 50 years + extension | 1x |
| Price per kg fuel (U / Th) | $4500 (5% enriched) | $50 | 90x |
| Energy output per kg fuel | 1 – 2 GWh (thermal) | 22 GWh* (thermal) | 15x |
| Construction time (GW plant) | 4 – 15 years | 6 – 18 months** | 10x |
| Electricity price | $60 – 120 MWh (e) | $20 – 40 MWh (e)** | 3x |

* To get all details, ask ChatGPT: Calculate the fission energy from one kg. of thorium in GWh thermal energy
** Remains to be proven, details available under NDA

copenhagen atomics

*Figure 17.  © Copenhagen Atomics 2024*

The development programme timeline for CA reactors plans to have them commercially available at scale from 2029. The construction time for a GW-sized plan would be around 6-18 months (speed equals cost savings). A likely key assumption is that the site is prepared and other infrastructure (roads, etc.) is installed.

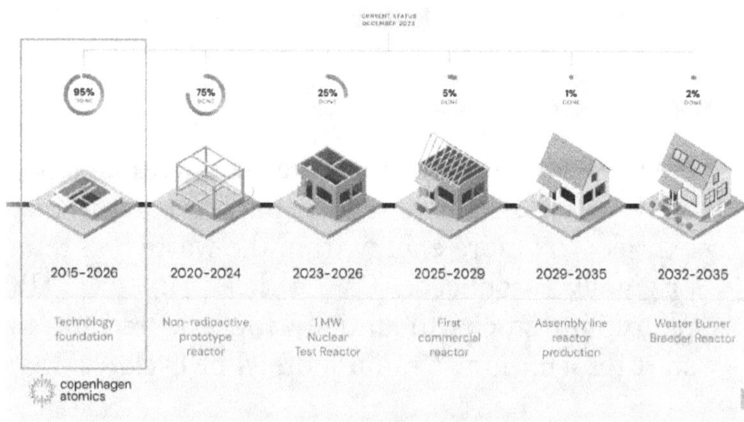


*Figure 18.  © Copenhagen Atomics*

Right now, Copenhagen Atomics needs a first site, and it also needs to find a way to fuel the reactor to start the Thorium reaction initially. The UK would be perfect because of the credibility that CA would gain for future orders. This provides an ideal opportunity to leverage a good deal, early involvement and commitment would help UK engineering firms bid for work and potentially site the manufacturing of the reactors in the UK. The UK should be preparing some of its existing old sites to host these plants, and we need to work together with CA to achieve regulatory approval of both the reactors and fuelling using PU or SNF waste plus question over transport security.

## Additional Sources of Revenue

One might think that the only source of revenue from a molten salt reactor would be electricity, but this would be wrong. There is a secondary use for the excess heat after the production of electricity that could be used in other industrial processes (for example, the production of ammonia for fertiliser) or even as a heat store to heat homes and premises directly.

The higher temperatures produced on an MSR over PWR can drive a gas turbine more than a steam turbine, and the excess heat can then continue for further processes requiring high temperatures and heating. Fast reactors are even more productive in this respect due to their higher temperatures. This provides a much more efficient use of the energy generated than is currently harvested from conventional thermal and existing nuclear.

One MSR developer, Moltex, has put forward a molten salt heat storage concept (to produce a grid reserve) to enable the reactor to supplement intermittent renewables. Hot nitrate salt at about 600°C is transferred to storage tanks, which are able to hold eight hours of reactor output at 2.5 GW thermal (as used in solar CSP plants). The heat store is said to add only £3/MWh to the levelised cost of electricity.

In addition to up-cycling the excess heat, which could provide another 10% of revenue, there also remain some very interesting by-products of the nuclear reaction. The first of these is tritium ($H_3$). This is frequently bled off existing reactors (usually as steam) and released into the atmosphere as it is only slightly radioactive and essentially harmless because it becomes rapidly diluted. However, pure tritium is a precious commodity that can be used in numerous applications, such as night vision equipment. The cost of Tritium is in excess of $30,000 per gram. World stock is only 20-30kg, and it is the raw material for fusion reactors, so I happily forecast that demand will grow. The annual tritium consumption of a fusion power plant operating at 1GW fusion power is c.55.6 kg per year or 152g per day.

Tritium is readily produced in reactors using Lithium-based salts (such as FLIBE), especially if the proportion of Li6 is increased. Expensive processing is required to purify the lithium in the salt to high levels of Li7 to inhibit tritium production. This purification process could be less exacting if the tritium could be collected and resold. Indeed, it would be possible to produce and collect economically significant amounts of tritium. The electric output of a 1 GW(e) plant in a day is worth about £120,000, and collecting half a gram of tritium daily would yield an additional 10% of income.

In addition to fission gases, various lanthanides and actinides are produced and found in the fuel salt. Some of these have valuable properties in treating cancer, and as they are not naturally occurring, they are scarce and thus valuable. These could also be separated and sold on the open market or purchased "internally" by the NHS. It is hard to put a firm value on this, but it could be a similar order of magnitude as the tritium, which is an additional 10% of revenue.

There is one additional source of revenue or a negative cost. If the new generation of reactors were initially fueled by nuclear waste or plutonium stocks, then we wouldn't have to pay to continue to store this. The generator company could be paid to take them and reprocess them into fresh fuel. MSRs are especially effective as reprocessing old fuel by dissolving it into molten salt is considerably simpler and cheaper than reprocessing it into new fuel rods.

Nuclear energy is cheaper than any intermittent renewable alternatives once you factor in reliability.

- Adopt at scale to achieve greater economy in the approval, build and operating phases.

- Remove and reduce bureaucratic red tape on the approval and planning cycle to reduce the time taken to get to operating status.

- Leverage the government's blue-chip credit rating to bring down the cost of finance.

- Advanced generation of MSR provides a unique set of benefits that reduce the operating and decommissioning costs.

- We could make it cheaper over its entire operating lifetime than a gas-fired plant.

# Chapter 7
# Implementing a Balanced Energy Strategy

I would like you to consider the world as it was about 120 years ago before electricity was in widespread use. We had coal and steam power, but machinery was large and industrial. There were few labour saving devices, lighting was poor and expensive, agriculture was manual, and food was expensive. Now consider your life today, there is almost no part of it that has not been completely transformed by either electricity or power from the internal combustion engine. The harnessing of fossil fuels to provide energy has irrevocably altered our lives, health and wealth for the better. Almost everything around you results from relatively cheap, reliable energy. Abundant energy equals prosperity.

If energy is the key to prosperity, let's take a quick reminder of where the UK is and where it is going. The UK has the 3rd most expensive electricity in the World. Only Denmark and Germany are higher, which has much to do with the latter shutting down several fully functioning, relatively new nuclear power plants in 2023 to burn more coal. It also has a lot to do with why Germany is currently in a recession / zero growth situation.

*Figure 19.  World Cost of Electricity [42]*

This means that an industry that is power intensive cannot be competitive and is shut down As has been happening (c.f. Port Talbot, etc). However, we don't stop needing these products. All that happens is we now import them from places like China, where they are manufactured from electricity invariably powered by more polluting coal.  Power is integral to industry. If it is expensive relative to elsewhere, it will not be able to compete and will shut down. It is that simple.  UK firms pay up to 4 times more for their energy than some in the US.

Recently, the heads of several large technology companies (Google, Microsoft and Oracle) have come right out and said that only nuclear power can drive the new data centres required to power AI. Only nuclear can produce sustained, reliable power at the required levels.  Failure to have this resource will mean these new data centres and supporting high-paid technology jobs will be placed in other countries.

Not only is our electricity currently the most expensive, but this will also worsen as we move the generating mix away from cheap CCGT and old nuclear plants toward more costly intermittent renewables.  Solar can be competitive with CCGT, but it is less reliable as it only delivers 10% of the installed power.  As discussed in Chapter 2, intermittent renewables cannot provide a sustainable and reliable grid because the amount of power storage for the frequent, lengthy winter periods of low wind and poor / zero sunlight is too expensive to be practical. Especially when added to already costly renewables.

Look at countries that don't have reliable power grids, generally third-world countries in Africa. This means that hospitals, public services, and businesses need their power backup and generating abilities, either at the public expense or the expense of other productive investments, thus depressing growth.  Then imagine your misery of not having power for several hours per day as the system suffers brownouts or total blackouts. Heating, cooking, washing, TV, and internet are all unavailable.  No first-world country has regular blackouts, but that doesn't mean it is not possible or even probable that it could happen. Executives from the Grid Electricity System Operator (ESO) have privately warned of blackouts by 2028 unless the South East pays more for power than other regions due to the shift to wind and solar.[43] However, this would effectively result in relegation to developing nation status.

Investors come to developing nations because of untapped and future potential. They won't invest in places in self-inflicted decline, making it harder to operate a business. There have been some attempts to alleviate the situation. A notable example is Morocco's combined wind/solar / battery farm (XLinks), which sends power via a high-voltage DC cable.  Somewhere, like Morocco, achieves considerably better solar efficiency than the UK and has relatively reliable coastal convection wind around dusk. This delivers power like "base load", i.e., always available. This is unproven and contentious.  The first phase is planned to deliver 1.8GW with a total of 3.6GW or 8% of our power requirement when completed.  In principle, I do not have any real problem with this project. Indeed, it seems more sane than some; relying on assets based in a foreign (African) country for your only *reliable* energy is risky. There is a long list of sovereign states that have suddenly decided to nationalise foreign-owned assets for their political purposes. Indeed, state actors have also cut or blown up undersea energy assets in war without being caught. A cable of this length is much more vulnerable than a short cable in the English Channel.

Meanwhile, the new Labour government will need to accelerate the UK's wind and solar charge to meet their shortened timescale of decarbonised grid by 2030. Energy consultants ICIS says they must secure up to 33GW (!!) in the next two years' auctions (2024 and 2025). A whopping £1.1bn budget hopefully delivers around 6GW in 2024 year's round. However, the funding may need three times greater to leverage the necessary scale. Arguably, the auction budget is not a "subsidy". The operating balance sheet allows the state to manage contracts for difference (CfD), where the state earns an arbitrage profit or loss depending on whether the market price of electricity is above or below the CfD strike price. If it is not to be a loss (or de facto subsidy), then the average price of electricity on the spot market when the wind and solar are generating will have to be above the CfD price. Given the predominant shift to these forms of power, with much potential excess supply available all at the same time, it is driving down the average price for wind or solar power compared to other forms of energy. This is also likely to increase the average price significantly at other times. Thus, I contend that it will be a massive taxpayer-funded subsidy. Without cheaper, *reliable* electrical energy, we are condemned to a poorer and colder future.

## Wishful Thinking & Procrastination

Fusion power, as the holy grail of all power generation, has created the perfect potential for those politicians and others wanting to avoid building nuclear power plants to procrastinate. They say Fusion Power is just around the corner, only another 5 or 10 years, so we don't need nuclear. A waste of money, let us invest in fusion, they say. We have poured billions of pounds into investigating and developing fusion power, going well beyond the obligations of various international schemes we have joined while almost completely stopping work on nuclear.

Developing fusion power is potentially worthy. It is one of those projects where there are breakthroughs, but it is always just another 5, 10 or 20 years away, depending on who you talk to. The scale of the engineering challenges involved in fusion power is two orders of magnitude greater (100 x) than those needing to be solved to bring cheap molten salt nuclear reactors online in only a handful of years. A technology as complex as this will be challenging to bring to commercial success and will have many teething issues.

Harnessing fusion power is just one of many excuses governments of all the main parties use to avoid making difficult and unpopular decisions. The primary reason that the UK stopped building nuclear power stations was the decisions taken in the late 1980s in the run-up to the privatisation of the electricity industry. At this time, North Sea gas was in full flow and would last another 40 years, and climate change wasn't really on the radar, so there was no imperative to build more nuclear power. However, procrastination has been the order of the day since 1997 (as Labour was elected) when we were looking at the replacements for the last generation of advanced gas reactors (AGR) that are now being decommissioned. Eventually, a decision in principle was made to replace the generation of AGR. Still, it took until 2012 to grant a site licence and until 2016 for the final decision to proceed with HPC.

Eventually, we proceeded with Hinckley Point when energy reliability was a critical issue, and it was obvious that something had to be done. However, by then, the nuclear industry in the UK had ceased to exist, and the design and build capabilities had withered to nothing, which has directly contributed to the cost overruns with HPC. It has, in turn, led to further dithering over Sizewell. In 2020, nuclear power generated 46 TWh of UK electricity, circa 15% of total electricity generation, and about half its 1998 peak of 91 TWh. Only in the energy crisis of 2022, when Russia invaded Ukraine and electricity prices were going through the roof, did we finally start to see a commitment to nuclear energy. However, as the crisis fades and a new government arrives, we are once again at risk of engaging in wishful thinking that intermittent renewables can solve all problems. The problems can only be solved if there is greater pressure on and consensus within the political class to prioritise energy prosperity and avoid grandstanding over green targets.

## What is a Balanced Energy Strategy

A balanced energy strategy would be one where all the generating sources are in harmony with one another and complementary to power demand. One where there would be sufficient reserves of capacity to meet peak demands no matter the environmental conditions.

A balanced energy strategy would produce affordable, abundant energy at stable long-term prices. Over the past few years, one of the manifest problems has been the wildly fluctuating electricity prices. This instability has created many problems both for businesses and consumers. Businesses have been driven to bankruptcy or closure by spiking prices. However, at least this can be seen and measured. Unseen is the damage that has been done to potential investment that would have funded growth, fueled the economy, grown taxes and welfare. If you risk your potential returns being destroyed by rising energy costs, you will not invest. Remember that energy prices have been in an uptrend for years, directly harming economic growth and higher taxation rates. Volatile prices can fuel inflation, affecting the investment potential for businesses.
It has also been a case of tightening belts or going without for consumers. Families face the choice of either heating or eating. High electricity prices lead directly to increased poverty levels, which naturally affect the most vulnerable elements of society.

Stable long-term electricity prices would fuel economic growth and jobs directly and indirectly. Directly by developing skilled, high-paying jobs in a nascent nuclear technology revival. Indirectly through better rates of economic growth.

The UK electorate has often been promised a green jobs bonanza, which has largely failed to materialise as much of the manufacturing of either wind turbines or solar has gone overseas. Of course, some installation and maintenance jobs have been created in some locations, but one cannot help but feel that this has been largely disappointing and was foreseeable. Investment in world-leading nuclear capabilities could quickly outstrip the number and overall quality of jobs going to wind and solar. These jobs would not easily be exported or outsourced from the UK for the most part.

Adopting advanced nuclear generation at scale would create a balanced energy-generating environment and has the following specific benefits:

- Stable and cheaper long-term and very long-term electric prices.

- Energy stability is free from price risk associated with fossil fuels or other imported materials.

- The security of the energy supply is not dependent on other countries.

- Creates high-quality, long-lasting engineering and manufacturing jobs (balancing our predominantly service economy).

- Directly and indirectly, it drives economic growth through investment.

- Potential siting of generating capacity closer to regions of demand requiring less grid infrastructure (e.g. pylons and other cabling).

- Demand balancing (load following) capabilities are absent in solar and wind.

## The Future is Nuclear

To decide how to adopt advanced nuclear to create stable and cheaper electricity, let us consider the sources of (nuclear) fuel. A golf ball-sized lump of thorium would provide enough energy for the entire lifetime needs of one person (including all energy we consume, such as healthcare, roads, etc). When mined, that Thorium costs $100 [source: Copenhagen atomics]. Thorium is one of the most abundant elements on Earth; it exists in every cubic metre of the Earth's crust. Existing mining operations (where THorium is a waste product) could provide enough for any conceivable demand.

In addition to this energy source, the UK sits on a metaphorical goldmine of 140 tonnes of Plutonium. This is valuable because it can initially fuel reactors that will become breeder reactors from Thorium/Uranium. Using this as a resource, rather than sitting around as an ongoing proliferation risk and general cost, must be a good thing. I don't accept proliferation arguments when the Plutonium is staying within the UK (already a nuclear power), and it would be much easier to disappear, steal or otherwise fall into the wrong hands sitting around than trying to extract it from a working nuclear reactor.

Furthermore, we are also sitting on large amounts of old Uranium nuclear waste fuel rods, which can be reprocessed and used in burner reactors. Enough waste already exists to be recycled in MSR, producing all the UK's power needs in a couple of generations. The same argument applies: it is better to deploy it usefully (96% of it is recyclable) than pay for it to sit around and try to find somewhere to bury it at vast expense.

The UK already has expertise in producing uranium-based solid fuel rods and fuel reprocessing. The planned investment in producing highly enriched low assay uranium (HALEU) for small reactors means we can proceed with 3rd generation PWR of a (small) modular design.

We have already discussed the expected benefits of repeatable modular design in driving down costs and timescales in Chapter 6. The result of the competitive process to decide which candidates will proceed to the final planning and build phase should be announced shortly. To deliver on the benefits of this, we must build quite a number of these reactors, though they should be clustered on a smaller number of sites. Rolls Royce is a domestic supplier with expertise in this field from its role as prime constructor for nuclear submarines (although the design is somewhat different).

Finally, we have a thriving research and development community that can be leveraged for next-generation reactor research. The UK is well placed to leverage our nuclear history to build the current and the next generation of reactors.

## Beyond the Renewables debate: An Action Plan for Scaling Nuclear

There are several areas where UK policymakers, regulators, and GBN need to take action to drive towards a balanced energy strategy featuring more nuclear power and less reliance on unreliable and usually expensive energy sources. Ultimately, the future will be advanced (4th generation +) reactors that will be safer, cheaper to build, economical to operate, and produce less waste. We must recognise this and implement plans and action to be among the first countries to deploy this technology.

### Research

Our first effort must be to fund collaboration between academia and industrial partners to drive research in the critical outstanding areas for MSR. These are

- Pumps and valves

- Primary heat exchanges

- Chemical processing

- Scaled-down Test reactors

If we diverted just a tiny fraction of what we are spending on fusion, we could take rapid steps forward with all these elements and thus drive the point at which a commercial reactor is produced. GBN could hold patents for successful inventions that could be licensed to commercial companies, which could be used to repay loans to the government and/or defray the costs of GBN.

Government progress on research is currently limited to HTGR. To help enable an Advanced Modular Reactor (AMR) demonstration by the early 2030s, the government has provided £55m development funding for two high-temperature gas reactor (HTGR) designs. Running until March 2025, these studies will undertake FEED+ (Front End Engineering Design and supporting activities) for the HTGR designs.

## Regulation (NRA)

As we have already discussed in Chapter 6, there is excellent scope for rationalising and reducing the overlap in regulation between different national and international bodies. Making some of these (trusted) bodies collaborative rather than competitive would speed the process, thus saving time and cost). This can only be achieved at a governmental level as most regulators are governed by statute/legislation. There has already been some discussion about the merits of this, but it needs to be formalised. I just want to note that we should not rely on this recognition being reciprocated, but that would be nice.

## Planning

In previous chapters, we discussed some of the issues around planning. The impact of these must be considered. The lengthy hurdles that private and public projects have to jump through with the attendant public inquiries and judicial reviews drive up the cost of projects to prohibitive levels, especially for private capital. However, state spending also faces the same barriers.

*"...the most important economic fact about modern Britain: that it is difficult to build almost anything, anywhere. This prevents investment, increases energy costs, and makes it harder for productive economic clusters to expand. This, in turn, lowers our productivity, incomes, and tax revenues." Foundations - why Britain has stagnated. [50]*

The planning requirements for "strategic importance" projects have already been somewhat reduced. However, many more pieces of legislation are creating onerous requirements, some from European environmental legislation, where exemptions could be carved out. The environmental impact assessment for Sizewell was 379,000 pages. How is that even possible or useful? What will be achieved? Pressure groups will just try to pick holes in it to launch judicial reviews or appeals. Do we want to do something critical and get on with it nationally, or do we not?

Any assessments should be prepared before that decision - to influence or inform it - not after the fact.

## Siting

3rd-gen PWR or small modular PWR still requires large reserves of water to provide cooling. Still, when it comes to siting new generation nuclear, there are not the same requirements to be near large amounts of water, thus giving more flexibility in the siting. However, we would want other critical considerations: make it easy to connect any new plants to the grid. We also have to consider the physical security of the plant and the transport links to bring in materials or deliver modular reactors.

Notwithstanding these considerations, the fact is that we already have 15 sites in the UK that would meet these requirements. These are the sites of old or existing nuclear power plants. Community acceptance rates in areas with these old sites are likely to be higher due to experience and having people/families who worked on the sites. Furthermore, they have a good grid and sufficient transport connections. On the other hand, several of these sites are in Scotland. With the expansion of wind power in Scotland (eating grid capacity) and opposition from the Scottish Parliament, we should exclude these four sites. Eight sites have been earmarked by the government, with two sites in development (Hinckley and Sizewell) and two being prepared.

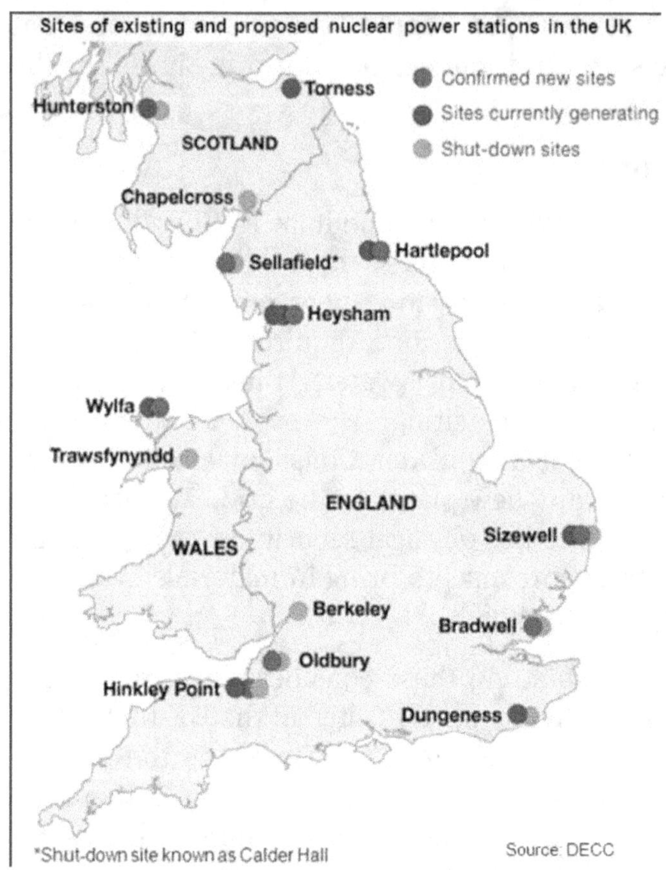


Figure 20. Nuclear Sites in the UK.  DECC

*"Wylfa on Ynys Mon (Anglesey) and Oldbury in Gloucestershire are now being brought under public ownership, with Great British Nuclear paying £160 million to acquire the two sites from previous owner Hitachi. In May 2024, the government confirmed that Wylfa is its preferred site for a third new gigawatt-scale development and opened an engagement exercise with interested technology vendors."* Nuclear AMRC

Three further sites are strong contenders: Berkeley, Dungeness and Winfrith (near the South Coast, the site of two research and development reactors connected to the grid). This would give us the ready potential for 11 sites. Dungeness was ruled out due to the supposed risk of rising sea levels. Given that the predicted acceleration in the rate of advance has not happened and has remained constant (at c. 3mm p.a.), we should look again.

## Organisation

The Office for Nuclear Regulation (ONR) is the independent regulator for the nuclear industry that approves designs and monitors safety compliance.

Great British Nuclear was set up in 2022/23 and will deliver the government's long-term nuclear programme and support the government's ambition to deliver up to 24GW of nuclear power in the UK by 2050. However, its remit had not been clarified by July 2024, and it is unclear how this will develop with the new Labour government setting up Great British Electric. However, it is clear that if we are to drive nuclear projects forward, we need somebody accountable for doing so. This makes it an excellent organisation to act as an umbrella for the proposed Special Purpose Vehicles we should set up for each nuclear facility.

The Civil Nuclear Constabulary (CNC) is responsible for security at civil nuclear sites within

5 km (3.1 miles) of site boundaries and for nuclear materials in transit.

The Nuclear Decommissioning Authority (NDA), formed in April 2005 under the Energy Act 2004, oversees and manages the decommissioning and clean-up of the UK's older Magnox power plants and the reprocessing facilities at Sellafield, which were transferred to its ownership from BNFL, and the former nuclear research and development facilities previously run by the UKAEA.

British Nuclear Fuels Ltd (BNFL).   The Future Nuclear Enabling Fund of up to £120 million will provide targeted support for new nuclear to address barriers to entry and will announce a shortlist of applications to begin pre-grant award due diligence.

## Financing

As we laid out in Chapter 6, we need a new financing model that encourages maximum efficiency and combines these elements to minimise financing costs. The CfD model becomes expensive to finance when the operator carries too much risk and the project becomes too large and complex; these costs/risks are passed on to the consumer.   Alternatively, in the RAB model, the operator carries too little risk and can incentivise inefficient and slow delivery (another cost to the consumer). We need a new hybrid model to slice and dice the risk, breaking it up and parcelling it out where it is cheapest and most efficiently managed. For the consumer to benefit from this approach, it is essential to have a competitive landscape for nuclear power, with multiple companies tendering to build and operate nuclear power plants. However, the ultimate and most outsized (primarily political) risks have to finally sit with the UK Treasury, as only the nation-state can bear and finance these sized risks economically.

## Leverage Industry

Leveraging the UK's industrial base to build a new generation of nuclear plants, tiny modular reactors (SMRs), and advanced nuclear designs presents a strategic opportunity to enhance energy security, reduce carbon emissions, and stimulate economic growth. The UK's industrial base, comprising a robust network of engineering expertise, manufacturing capabilities, and a skilled workforce, positions the country as a leader in the global nuclear renaissance.

The UK has a rich history in nuclear technology, from developing early reactors to operating a fleet of advanced gas-cooled reactors (AGRs). This legacy provides a deep reservoir of knowledge and technical expertise that can be harnessed for the next generation of nuclear plants. The UK's nuclear supply chain includes world-class engineering firms, construction companies, and research institutions well-positioned to support the design, manufacture, and deployment of SMRs and advanced reactors.

Collaboration between government, industry, and academia is crucial to advancing nuclear technologies. The UK can leverage its industrial base by fostering partnerships that bring together different sectors to innovate and overcome technical challenges. For instance, the UK's Catapult centres, designed to bridge the gap between research and industry, can play a pivotal role in developing new reactor designs, improving safety features, and reducing costs. Additionally, by promoting public-private partnerships, the government can ensure that the nuclear industry remains competitive globally.

SMRs offer several advantages over traditional large-scale nuclear reactors, including lower capital costs, shorter construction times, and greater flexibility in deployment. With its precision engineering capabilities, the UK's manufacturing sector is well-suited to produce the modular components required for SMRs. Furthermore, the UK can lead in the global SMR market by investing in research and development, streamlining regulatory processes, and creating domestic manufacturing and export incentives.

What is not often fully appreciated is that a substantial part of the cost of a nuclear power station design is the cost of developing and rigorously testing the software that monitors and controls all the processes. As with all software, the initial development cost is high, but the cost of replication and further deployment is negligible. Therefore, producing many SMRs will enable companies to develop software once and then leverage this over many implementations.

Beyond SMRs, advanced nuclear designs such as Generation IV reactors and fusion energy represent the future of low-carbon energy. The UK can leverage its industrial base by supporting companies developing these technologies. This could include providing financial incentives for innovation, supporting workforce training programs to ensure a pipeline of skilled labour, and facilitating international collaborations to share knowledge and reduce development timelines.

The UK could be at the forefront of a new era in nuclear energy by leveraging its industrial base. Through strategic investments in SMRs and advanced reactors, the UK can meet its energy and environmental goals and position itself as a global leader in nuclear technology. This will require a coordinated effort across industry, government, and academia, but the rewards for economic growth, energy security, and environmental sustainability are worth the effort.

## Design for Decommissioning

One of the significant costs of nuclear has turned out to be decommissioning. Whenever the anti-nuclear lobby mentions outrageous decommissioning costs for the nuclear programme, 60% of that total is for dealing with *just* the Sellafield / Windscale reprocessing site rather than individual power plants.  The design and build of early reactors did not factor in decommissioning, and the result has been oversized costs. However, while these costs are inherent, they can be reduced. These costs can be significantly reduced by factoring in how each element will be maintained and then eventually decommissioned during the design phase. The EPRs being constructed at HPC and Sizewell have been designed around this principle of reducing decommissioning costs. This should be considered in all future designs approved for the UK.

# Chapter 8 - Summary and Conclusion

When I undertook to write this book, it was to alert the reader to the disingenuousness of the debate around our path to "Net Zero". If politicians of all parties have not been lying for the past 25 years, then they have been wilfully ignorant. The current consensus, or dangerous groupthink, has meant that there has not been much debate around Net Zero. Prime ministers, from Blair onwards, dithered on energy policy. Tony Blair oversaw the Climate Change Act (CCA) 2008. Theresa May the 2050 target amendment. We are one of just a handful of nations to have bound ourselves legislatively. There has literally been an energy review or whitepaper launched by the government every few years (2002, 2003, 2006, 2007, etc), and nearly all of these have simply "kicked the can down the road". In each case, we have primarily proceeded with an overwhelming reliance on wind and solar projects to meet our needs combined with a dose of "something will turn up" (e.g. cheap battery storage, green hydrogen or carbon capture).

All administrations agreed that a reduction in fossil fuel was required, but there needed to be a proper plan to replace the gigawatts of power lost by decommissioning perfectly serviceable power stations. All this is forecasted while there are considerable increases in electricity demand for new electric cars and heat pumps and the substitution of gas or coal power currently used in high-energy industrial processes.

Meanwhile, some of our international competitors, notably China and India, have accelerated the building of new fossil fuel power stations even as we have been expensively subsidising the process of decommissioning and transitioning to intermittent renewables. I mention India and China because the scale of what they do matters - 2.7 billion people versus 70 million—roughly 40 times more. We could achieve net zero tomorrow, eliminating less than 1% of global emissions. China and India are increasing their $CO_2$ emissions by this amount each year.

What I find especially galling is that this has been dressed up as a moral crusade of the righteous, enlightened, liberal West who need to set an example to the benighted developing world so that they will follow our example. Meanwhile, non-G7 countries have been pretty clear that they will continue their development as they see fit, and there is no way that "we" will preach to them about being "Green" while pulling up the drawbridge. It is clearly viewed as hypocritical. Both Narendra Modi and Xi Jinping are nationalists who view the UK, its colonial past, and our recent moral conversion with some justified suspicion. They remember the morality and oppression of the Raj and the China Opium

Wars, and why wouldn't they? They are not in any way inclined to see the UK as setting a moral example that they are prepared to follow. Suppose we wish to beggar ourselves by accelerating our move to Net Zero, not their problem, their opportunity instead to export more things to us that we no longer make.

People make much of the amount of wind and solar power that China is installing, which is impressive. However, they are simultaneously adding new coal and gas plants to their inventory at equal speed to keep up with insatiable demand. Their conversion to renewables has as much to do with their own agenda to reduce pollution as with the fight against $CO_2$. They also play to their mercantilist instincts to build the capacity to dominate these industries, just as they have done with electric cars.

 Meanwhile, in the UK, "Winter is coming" with the first Dunkelflaute. That's the term used in the energy industry to refer to a period of anti-cyclonic high pressure and calm that we experience in winter when it is freezing, but the blades of the wind turbines won't turn, and the Sun hardly rises above the horizon for more than a couple of hours. This is when the risk of blackouts rises, and we need to curb demand by restricting electricity usage to both industry and consumers (who receive discounts by agreeing to this).

While the grid regulator (ESO) is trying to avoid blackouts, politicians in Westminster are grandstanding at each COP and talking about the thousands of "green" jobs, how we will be the "Saudi Arabia of wind", and how they will "save" £300 yearly on our energy bills, while not drilling for any more gas or oil. We will do all this by 2030; however, doing things faster invariably means that they cost even more.

As Gary Smith, leader of the GMB Union, told The Spectator, "Communities up and down the East Coast can see wind farms, but they can't point to the jobs. Instead of decent jobs with decent salaries", he says, "it's usually a man in a rowing boat, sweeping up the dead birds."

When "green" jobs are paid for in part by green levies and assisted through red tape on business investment, we risk distorting the economy by misallocating capital and resources to signal political allegiance rather than prioritising productivity.

As Milton Freedman noted, changing shovels for spoons creates the need for more jobs, but not ones that make progress and increase productivity, rather the opposite.

The new government has promised that GB Energy will save us £300 on our electricity bills. This is based on a single study (pre-covid) using favourable assumptions about the cost of wind continuing to fall. The budget for GB energy is supposedly being funded by "windfall taxes" on fossil fuel companies. The decision to raise the rate of taxation on North Sea profits to 78% and cancel most allowances will increase the amount raised this year and next.  However, undermining future investment will hammer it flat after this, leaving GB Energy devoid of its £8.3bn budget.

## UK Energy Strategy:  Where we are - the problem

Government figures show that UK energy production, including gas, oil and electricity, fell 8.3% to a record low in 2023, while we imported a record 41% of these items in 2023, up from 37% in 2022.  UK electricity prices have risen faster than almost any other developed country since 2019, the International Energy Agency (IEA) has found.

Soaring wholesale costs and an increase in net zero levies have led to British households paying more for their power, as they now face the third highest prices in Europe.  In just the last year, the price of electricity in the UK rose by 19% and has doubled since 2019, while in the US, prices have increased by just 5% a year since 2019. According to a report from the House of Commons library, the UK's spike has been driven by taxes and levies linked to net zero.  In the UK in 2023, taxes and levies comprised 17% of electricity and 7% of gas bills."

The IEA report warns that high electricity prices across the UK and Europe will undermine competitiveness: "Despite an estimated 50% price decline in 2023 versus 2022, energy-intensive industries in the region continued to face far higher electricity costs compared with the US and

China in the aftermath of Russia's invasion of Ukraine."

We are paying a lot more for our electricity than we were due to our current obsession with decarbonising the grid. However, this is not the only problem, as we discussed in Chapter 2.

If we have a grid based on intermittent renewables, we cannot just consider the cost of generation. We have to add the cost of energy storage or other types of backup. The other alternative is to build so many wind and solar farms that we have enough power at the worst of times and a super-abundance of it at most other times, both horribly inefficient and impossible. This is because the weather patterns we are guarding against may affect not just the whole UK but large areas of the continent, too, so no matter how many turbines you have, if none of them are turning, you are sunk.

All energy storage solutions are horrendously expensive. Lithium batteries, for example, can cost around six times as much as generating it in the first place. We need to bear in mind that Dunkelflaute systems can stay in place for up to three weeks, and periods of five days are not uncommon. Therefore, we would also need storage batteries at an unimaginable scale. Californian studies suggest a cost of $15 trillion (£11.5 trillion) for that state alone, with replacement every 10-12 years, and they *don't* suffer from Dunkelflaute systems, so they only need to have storage for hours or a day or two.

The plundering of Africa and South America to yield the minerals required for batteries has not even been calculated. Other battery solutions are not yet commercially available and often involve the trade-off of cheaper cost for (much) greater size. Remember, land is also valuable and demands a commercial return, so size is a problem unless you build up.

Using gas as a backup means building dedicated gas-fired plants designed to be fired up and down at short notice rather than the more economical CCGT plant. These gas power stations spend a lot of time sitting idle, which is an inefficient use of resources (capital) and pushes up the unit cost of generation.

With many of Britain's offshore wind farms being built far from the main areas of demand, such as the Midlands and the South, massive investment in grid infrastructure will also be required to ensure power can be efficiently moved around the country. The current system largely ignores the realities of how much power can be transferred from North to South, owing to physical limits on the capacity of transmission cables. It also forces the ESO to balance the system to keep the lights on, for example, by paying wind farms to stop generating in Scotland and gas-fired plants in the South to switch on. The ESO must often make these decisions within a one-hour window and at considerable expense to consumers. A recent study by FTI Consulting estimated that these "constraint" payments will reach £2bn in 2030 and around £5bn in 2035. [47]

## UK Energy Strategy - Where do we want to be

*Cheap, clean, and secure energy is not pursued as an end in itself. It is essential for enabling economic growth. Businesses and jobs in all sectors are dependent on energy. Britain led the world with the industrial revolution, off the back of a plentiful supply of coal. A future of abundant and clean energy will help to boost our economic prosperity, attract future investment and support our industrial heartlands. The cheaper our energy, the greater the competitive advantage we have.*     Powering Up Britain: Energy Security Plan HMSO March 2023 [7]

It has taken a long time and the energy crisis of 2022 to recognise the need for cheap, abundant, reliable energy, after spending the previous 20 years heading in the opposite direction. It is still unclear how these words are being translated into action, it seems the new government has reverted to path of renewables from horizon to horizon.

Accepting that decarbonising the grid is a relatively settled objective across the UK political spectrum, even if there has been some debate about the scale of the emergency and the speed at which we need to proceed.  Given the cost of renewables with energy storage, additional transmission infrastructure, and capacity payments, what are the realistic alternatives to these if we want to decarbonise the grid?

The criteria the alternatives need to meet are reliable sources of power generation, based in the UK (not imported), not subject to short-term price fluctuations, that can also "load follow" to balance the renewables on the grid. These generation sources should be able to be deployed close to the sources of demand to reduce the need for transmission infrastructure.

Our geography and geology dictate that we don't have ready sources of geothermal or hydroelectric power (the most plausible sites for these have already been utilised). Tidal power still needs to be commercially harnessed, although it is theoretically possible, and we have been looking into it for 60 years.

Can we be optimistic about nuclear fusion? Recent "breakthroughs" have been misleading, ignoring the vast energy required to power the plant. The technology needs to improve by orders of magnitude before more energy comes out than goes in. It's also worth noting that people talk about nuclear fusion power as though it would be free from fission's radiation and waste problems; this is emphatically not the case. Worthwhile fusion power has been supposedly imminent for more than half a century, and it's liable to be a very long time before it arrives. We should not put off building nuclear fission capacity to wait for it.

Realistically, nuclear fission is the only solution that meets all the criteria and can be delivered at scale in line with, or close to, our required timescales. With only nine reactors remaining, it is hard to remember Britain was once a pioneer in nuclear power. Decades of decline have meant the UK has fallen rapidly behind in the global atomic generation, jeopardising the country's energy security in the process. However, the World Nuclear Association (WNA) reports reveal how far other countries have forged ahead. China is set to build over 90 nuclear reactors by 2035, over which period the UK will complete just one. The WNA said that the gulf is despite Britain boasting a high-quality construction industry, which blamed the drop-off on poor decision-making by successive governments. Its latest report on the global nuclear sector shows that China currently has 56 reactors in operation, 30 under construction, with plans for another 60 by 2035.

The last two government administrations have confirmed a target for *new* nuclear power of 24 GW by 2040 as part of a strategy for ensuring energy "security". This does not seem overly ambitious when seen against the (July 2024) target of 60 GW of new electric by 2030 as part of Labour's plan. Given the issues inherent in renewables that we have discussed at length, it is only cost-effective for these sources to provide less than 50% of the capacity on the grid at any time. This amount (50%) is based on the IEA view about the exponential cost increase of balancing the grid with levels of renewables above this threshold.

Suppose the projected energy demand by 2040 is a total of 96 GW [48]. In that case, we should have a target of 48 GW (say by 2050) of nuclear to keep renewables to 50% and manage the cost of stabilising the grid (assuming no other non-intermittent and reliable carbon-free power sources). Even this does not answer the question of what to do about the other 48 GW of demand when there is no wind or sun.

## The nuclear option

As well as being imperative, there are several advantages to building lots of new nuclear capabilities. According to the International Energy Agency, a mind-boggling 370,000 miles of cable must be laid or upgraded to high-voltage cables to deliver renewables by 2050. As new nuclear capacity can be built where sites and infrastructure already exist, there are a lot of pylons that won't need to be constructed and blot the landscape.

If we build larger quantities of nuclear, we will achieve better economies of scale. This should be realised in many ways, from the physical manufacture (of reactors, pumps, heat exchangers) to building the software. As we saw with wind, once you start ramping up capabilities, the price tends to drop; of course, this particular trend has been derailed by rising prices for everything else. There should also be better opportunities to create efficiencies in manufacturing reactors rather than building them, such as SMR, versus a few very large reactors.

When considering what type of reactors to build, we must also consider how to build consensus and overcome objections. The additional advantages of molten salt reactors, liquid fuel over solid fuel, thorium over uranium, and potential cost advantages should guide us down this path over the medium term. The greater implicit safety of these designs (all nuclear designs are safe, but some are superior to others), with less waste and less nuclear material moving around, helps overcome these objections. We should be backing research into these reactors to finalise the designs for commercial use before the end of the decade. We should be helping these companies by preparing policies and procedures for reusing old solid fuel nuclear waste and plutonium to be ready to power up new generations of breeder reactors and waste burners.

As ever with nuclear, the main hurdle is regulatory. US developer NuScale recently secured certification from the US Nuclear Regulatory Commission (NRC) but said the process ran from 2008 to 2020, cost half a billion dollars and generated two million pages of documentation. And that certification only applies in the US – NuScale would have to go through it again if someone wanted to deploy its technology in the UK or elsewhere. The UK Government has said it intends to cooperate with trusted national regulators, and this would be an excellent place to start. If the technology is good enough for the NRC, it should be good enough for the UK and vice versa (of course, site-specific approvals must still be on a case-by-case basis, but even this needs streamlining).

## Overcoming the anti-nuclear Luddites

Once again, we return to overturning the four main objections postulated by the anti-nuclear lobby.

- Safe - no risk of nuclear accidents. Nuclear power is already the safest form of power generation, except solar, for deaths caused per TWh generated. Safer than wind or fossil fuel generation. However, new 4th generation nuclear designs have passive safety features that cannot suffer meltdowns or, explosions or leaks seen in the past. They don't use pressure or water for cooling.

- Tiny quantities of radioactive Waste - new generation nuclear can burn old radioactive waste, thus reducing the historic problems. They also burn nuclear fuel much more efficiently, burning up to 96% of the fuel introduced rather than something of the order of 10% in old reactors, which left 90% of it as waste.

- Nuclear Weapons. The by-products from modern civil reactors are not suitable for nuclear weapons programmes. The honest facts are that it is simply impractical to go from using civil nuclear fuel or products from 4th gen reactors to build atomic bombs. Going straight to purpose-built enrichment is easier than using civil fuel or waste to get to a bomb. Furthermore, we can use 4th gen nuclear to burn old UK stocks of plutonium (rather than used to make bombs), turning a problem into a valuable resource for starting up breeder reactor cycles using Thorium.

- Cheaper Electricity - advanced 4th generation and small modular reactors can deliver cheaper power than those generated by huge multi-gigawatt EPR plants like Hinkley Point and Sizewell, which are too monolithic, complex, and costly to build. Using water at pressure in an EPR for cooling creates too many safety issues that need multiple levels of mitigation, making it less cost-effective. New startup companies are backing molten salt and other advanced designs to deliver power at prices less than wind and solar with storage. These startups are forecasting prices of £40 MWh (without subsidies and including dealing with waste and decommissioning), which is significantly cheaper than offshore wind or comparable with solar but without taking over vast swathes of the countryside.

## Building Public Acceptance

We have now been over the standard objections to nuclear power put forward by the anti-nuclear lobby.  These objections play on the fears of the public, who naturally mistrust things they don't understand and cannot see.

You can never please all the people all of the time, but to boost the widespread consensus behind nuclear, we need to have organised campaigns in the following areas:

·       Grassroots advocacy and education

·       Public activism to spur government support

·       Lobbying policymakers for new-generation MSR adoption

Current polling suggests that support for nuclear power has been slowly rising, and it is at a healthy level, but we need to take it further. In a 2021 YouGov poll, 65% of those surveyed said nuclear power should play a role in the country's climate policy, and 12% expressed strong anti-nuclear sentiment, while 46% were aware that nuclear power is a low-carbon energy source. Crushing the "it's too expensive" cost argument would be a clincher.

## A Final Word

While the government's commitment to 24GW of new nuclear generating capacity is welcome, there is no moment to lose if we seize the initiative from just producing another generation of PWR and leap forward to 4th generation MSR.

The power generation and energy security business is a long-term game that consumes large quantities of capital. Hence, there is inertia and cleaving to the 'safe' path that the public is comfortable with (i.e., intermittent renewables). The new target of decarbonising the grid by 2030 makes it even more pressing because of the lead time to commission new large-scale nuclear plants. However, we should remember that offshore wind projects can take ten years to complete and that there are now constraints on delivering these faster (such as a shortage of specialist ships to install large offshore turbines - the lead time on these ships alone is years.

Striking out with small modular reactors and molten salt reactors will take a level of adventurism and risk-taking that is not readily associated with the risk averse decision making of the state. Energy policy and specific decisions to commission new power generation are purely political. Suppose we wish to leverage the full benefits of new-generation nuclear fission. In that case, we need a popular movement to drive political change, just as the green and anti-nuclear movements have pushed us down an extreme route of intermittent renewables.

## Author's note

Thank you for reading my book. I very much hope you enjoyed it and found it informative. You may be aware that Amazon reviews are critical for independent authors; without these, my work will never be seen, that is just the way the system works. I would like to ask you to spend two minutes to leave a review for me, and be assured I personally read all my reviews. Your review can have a massive social influence on who will read my book. If you have never left a review before, just give one or two points around your main impressions and what you enjoyed. **Thank you so much. Click on the Link below or scan the QR code:**

https://www.amazon.co.uk/dp/B0DKTH8694/review

# Glossary of Terms

AC - Alternating Current

AGR - Advanced Gas-cooled Reactor

AMR - Advanced Modular Reactor

BNFL - British Nuclear Fuels Ltd

CA - Copenhagen Atomics

CCA  - Climate Change Act

CCGT - Combined-Cycle Gas Turbine

CfD: Contracts for Difference

CNC - Civil Nuclear Constabulary

CO2: Carbon Dioxide

CPI - Consumer Prices Index

DC - Direct Current

EdF  - Elecricite de France

EPR - European Pressurised water Reactor

ESO - Electricity System Operator

FLiBe  - Flouride (F) salt containing Lithium (Li)
& Beryllium (Be)

FLiNaK  - Salt comprised of Fluoride Lithium Sodium
 & Potassium .

FP - Fission products

GBN - Great Britsh Nuclear

GW - Gigawatt

GWe: Giga Watt electric

GWh - Gigawatt-hour

HPC - Hinckley Point C

HTGR - High Temperature Gas Reactor

IAEA - International Atomic Energy Agency

IEA - International Energy Agency

IMF - International Monetary Fund

JRC - European Joint Research Centre

LCOE - Levelised Cost of Electricity

LFTR: Liquid Fluoride Thorium Reactor

MCSFR - Molten Chloride Salt Fast Reactor

MeV - Mega Electron Volts

MSBR - Molten Salt Breeder Reactor

MSFR - Molten Salt Fast Reactor

MSR: Molten Salt Reactor

MSRE - Oak Ridge (USA) trial Molten Salt Reactor

MW - Megawatt

MWh: Megawatt Hour

NAO: National Audit Office

NDA - Nuclear Decommissioning Authority

OCGT - Open-Cycle Gas Turbine

OECD - Organisation Economic Cooperation & Development

ORNL - Oak Ridge National Laboratory

Pa-233 - Protactinium 233

PBHTGR - Pebble Bed High-Temperature Gas-Cooled Reactors

PFI - Private Finance Initiative

PPP - Public / Private Partnership

Pu-239 - Plutonium-239

PV - Photovoltaic

PWR: Pressurised Water Reactor

RAB - Regulated Asset Base

RWe: A large European energy company

SMR - Small modular Reactor

SMR - Small Modular Reactor

SNF - Spent Nuclear Fuel

SPV - Special Purpose (financing) Vehicle

Th-232 - Thorium-232

TTT - Thames Tideway Tunnel project

TWh - Terawatt Hour

U-235 - Uranium-235

U-238 - Uranium-238

# References

---


References are supplied in the order of first appearance in the text

[1]https://world-nuclear.org/information-library/nuclear-fuel-cycle/nuclear-wastes/radioactive-wastes-myths-and-realities.aspx

[2]https://world-nuclear.org/nuclear-essentials/what-is-nuclear-waste-and-what-do-we-do-with-it.aspx

[3] *Environ. Sci. Technol.* 2011, 45, 15, 6237–6238

[4]https://www.nationalgrid.com/stories/energy-explained/how-will-our-electricity-supply-change-future

[5]https://www.telegraph.co.uk/business/2023/10/25/electricity-prices-rise-70pc-pay-wind-farms-energy/

[6]https://www.theguardian.com/environment/2011/jun/23/thorium-nuclear-uranium

[7] Powering up Britain: Energy Security Plan HM Government March 2023

[8]https://en.wikipedia.org/wiki/Wind_power_in_the_United_Kingdom

[9]https://www.equinor.com/news/202310-dogger-bank

[10]https://www.renewableuk.com/news/643056/UK-Offshore-Wind-pipeline-nears-100GW-as-Global-pipeline-tops-1.23TW.htm

[11] https://www.dnv.com/article/can-the-uk-achieve-its-50-gw-offshore-wind-target-by-2030--224379

[12]https://www.power-technology.com/news/vattenfall-halts-offshore-wind-project

[13] Offshore Wind Net Zero Investment Roadmap, HM Government, March 2023

[14] https://orsted.com/en/insights/the-fact-file/is-offshore-wind-power-reliable

[15]https://www.nao.org.uk/wp-content/uploads/2017/06/Hinkley-Point-C.pdf

[16]https://www.iea.org/commentaries/critical-minerals-threaten-a-decades-long-trend-of-cost-declines-for-clean-energy-technologies

[17] Digest of UK Energy Statistics (DUKES) produced by the Department for Energy Security & Net Zero (DESNZ). July 2023

[18]https://ember-climate.org/insights/commentary/uk-spent-350m-on-new-gas-power-despite-nearing-fossil-phase-out/

[19]https://www.ewea.org/wind-energy-basics/faq/

[20]https://www.telegraph.co.uk/business/2023/11/16/coutinho-boost-subsidies-wind-farm-projects-auction-flop/

[21] National Grid Electricity market reform body.
https://www.emrdeliverybody.com/sitepages/home.aspx

[22]https://www.statista.com/statistics/494425/death-rate-worldwide-by-energy-source/

[23]IAEA Converter Reactor Alternatives, Davis W.K. 1975

[24] IAEA Technical Report Series 489: Status of Molten Salt Reactor Technology.

 November 2023

[25] Gen IV International forum  IAEA Webinar 73. Dr J. Krepel

[26] The corrosion effects of neutron activation of 2LiF-BeF2 (FLiBe) . Vegari, Scarlet, Hayes , Fratoni.  Nuclear Materials and Energy.  March 2023.

[27] Civil Nuclear: roadmap to 2050   Published Jan 2024  HMSO

[28] Guidance on Development costs and the nuclear regulated asset based model. November 2022. DESNZ, HMSO

[29]https://www.nao.org.uk/press-releases/hinkley-point-c/

[30] Mind the Gap: Exploring Britain's energy crunch, Public First, 2024

[31]        https://namrc.co.uk/intelligence/uk-new-build/

[32]          https://www.qub.ac.uk/schools/queens-business-school/news/WhyPrivateFinanceInitiativeswereaDeeplyFlawedFinancingModel.html

[33]https://www.infrastructureinvestor.com/how-pfi-or-bust-went-bust/

[34]https://www.ippr.org/media-office/revealed-investment-in-uk-is-lowest-in-g7-for-third-year-in-a-row-new-data-shows

[35]https://www.economicsobservatory.com/financing-uk-rail-infrastructure-how-does-today-compare-with-the-past#:~:text=In%20comparison%2C%20HS2%20was%20funded,rail%20companies%20to%20secure%20funding.

[36]https://www.edfenergy.com/sites/default/files/V2%20C05%20Decommissioning%20of%20Hinkley%20Point%20C.pdf

[37]https://www.gov.uk/government/publications/hinkley-point-c-funded-decommissioning-programme

[38]https://assets.publishing.service.gov.uk/media/6556027d046ed400148b99fe/electricity-generation-costs-2023.pdf

[39]https://www.eia.gov/outlooks/aeo/pdf/electricity_generation.pdf

[40]https://energy.ec.europa.eu/system/files/2020-10/final_report_levelised_costs_0.pdf

[41]https://medium.com/generation-atomic/the-hinkley-point-c-case-is-nuclear-energy-expensive-f89b1aa05c27

[42]https://worldpopulationreview.com/country-rankings/cost-of-electricity-by-country

[43]https://www.telegraph.co.uk/business/2024/08/07/power-chiefs-fear-net-zero-blackouts-in-london/

[44] Pfenninger, Stefan; Keirstead, James (15 August 2015). "Renewables, nuclear, or fossil fuels? Scenarios for Great Britain's power system considering costs, emissions and energy security". *Applied Energy*. : 83–93.

[45]https://www.lastenergy.com/blog/financing-nuclear-in-the-uk-the-regulated-asset-base-rab-model-vs-contract-for-differences-cfd#:~:text=At%20its%20best%2C%20the%20RAB,developers%20to%20overspend%20on%20construction.

[46]https://www.itf-oecd.org/sites/default/files/dp_2016-01_makovsek_and_veryard.pdf

[47]https://www.telegraph.co.uk/business/2024/08/07/power-chiefs-fear-net-zero-blackouts-in-london/

[48]https://www.gov.uk/government/publications/british-energy-security-strategy/british-energy-security-strategy

[49]https://adelsfors.se/2024/05/27/adding-storage-to-windsolar-to-get-a-firm-output/#:~:text=This%20is%20only%2020%25%20in,is%20needed%2C%20around%20550%20GWh.

[50] Foundations - why Britain has Stagnated. 2024  Southwood, Hughes and Bowman

https://ukfoundations.co/

www.ingramcontent.com/pod-product-compliance
Lightning Source LLC
Chambersburg PA
CBHW051559250726
48653CB00004BA/1233